# MARIJUANA
# Made Simple

## A Beginner's Guide to Growing Like A Pro

### by Mediman

GREEN CANDY PRESS

Marijuana Made Simple: A Beginner's Guide To Growing Like A Pro

Published by Green Candy Press

San Francisco, CA

www.greencandypress.com

ISBN 978-1-931160-88-9

Photography: Mediman, David Strange, Stoned Rosie, Critical Jack
Cover photo © Andre Grossman

This book contains information about illegal substances specifically the plant Cannabis Sativa and its derivative products. Green Candy Press would like to emphasize that cannabis is a controlled substance in North America and throughout much of the world. As such, the use and cultivation of cannabis can carry heavy penalties that may threaten an individual's liberty and livelihood.

The aim of the Publisher is to educate and entertain. Whatever the Publisher's view on the validity of current legislation, we do not in any way condone the use of prohibited substances.

Printed in China by Oceanic Graphic Printing.

Massively distributed by P.G.W.

*You only get out what you put in.*

—M.F.B.

# CONTENTS

# Acknowledgments

I would like to thank my Mom and Dad for always supporting my medical marijuana use and growing; all of my friends who put up with me on a regular basis, especially Paul Pipe, Draygun, and Calum. Special thanks to NYPD and T. Dubya, for getting me started with my first garden and getting me involved with medical marijuana, plus always being great mentors and friends.

I would also like to thank the following for all their support and donations:

London Compassion Society
London, Ontario, Canada
londoncompassionsociety.com

Indoor Gardener
"We Turn Your Thumb GREEN!"
207 Exeter Rd.  Unit "D"
London, Ontario, Canada
N6L 1A4, 519-652-4224
indoorgardener.ca

Organic Traveller
London, Ontario, Canada
519-432-HEMP (4367)

# Introduction

## ■ About the author

My name is Mediman, and I was born with a rare genetic disease (1 case in 60,000) called Wilson's. Wilson's disease gives you genes in your liver that will not allow the body to remove copper, which is in everything you eat and drink. There are two types of Wilson's disease, neuro and gastro; I have both, but the neurological side is more prominent. I grew up unaware that I was suffering from this disease, but I was well aware that my brain did not run the same as everyone else's. I was extremely hyperactive and very disorganized, with a fast pace of thought that resulted in me being very misunderstood by my peers and family. A normal brain is designed to run two to three thoughts at a time, at a normal pace. A neuro Wilson's brain is designed to run seven to eight thoughts at a time, at a high pace, fueled by the copper that is being deposited in the brain rather than expelled out of the body. I took in so much information at a high speed that as a child I would speak with my own abbreviated language; most of the time people did not understand it, and judged me accordingly.

When I was fourteen, I smoked marijuana for the first time; the effects were overwhelming. Smoking marijuana allowed me to collect my thoughts and keep them organized at a normal pace. I continued to smoke it every day, which turned me into a completely different person—my friends and family thought I just finally started to show maturity, and did not know I was using marijuana to keep things under control. By the time I was eighteen, I started to have physical health problems with my liver, which was failing by the time I was twenty-two. I spent over two years being tested, over and over again, from doctor to doctor, until I was finally diagnosed with Wilson's disease. By this time, I had copper poisoning all over my body and in my bloodstream, and the removal process would take decades. I would not be able to

survive this process, leaving me what they deemed "terminally" ill. I became a legalized medical marijuana user a few years after that by my government and started to grow and use my own supply. My main concern was that I was using the purest and healthiest marijuana I could grow, which I believe was the key to surviving six years of severe metal poisoning, poisoning which made me vomit to the point of dry heaving all day, every day. Eventually, after a good eight years of being seriously ill, I survived enough copper removal to bring me to non-life-threatening levels. Without the consistent, pure, high-grade everyday use of the medical marijuana I was growing and using, I would not have been able to survive on my own.

## ■ About the book

Before I was diagnosed with Wilson's disease, I was a technical specialist for a major computer networking and cable manufacturer. Part of my job was to design as many new products as possible for the industry, writing my own owner's manuals for each product. In the 1990s, explaining how to use computer products and install them correctly without any problems was very difficult, but I would eliminate as many instructions as possible and explain the process very directly, removing unnecessary information that might confuse or overwhelm a general user. This is what I have done when creating this growing system. I have eliminated the most common problems people have when trying to learn how to grow and use marijuana, and have developed the most fail-proof method of growing possible: anyone in the world could easily understand and execute this process, leaving them with clean, pure, very high-grade marijuana first time out. In addition, I show how to keep growers and their homes as safe as possible.

There are many variables when growing a crop of marijuana; if any one of those variables is changed, it will alter your final outcome. In order for this growing system to work, you must follow everything I say exactly. Practice this growing system until you have it down pat—then you will be in a position to start changing variables of the growing process to your liking. My goal for the book is to improve your medical marijuana experience by showing you how to grow and use clean, high-grade marijuana. Hopefully, if the book is a success, it will force the people growing low-grade, dirty street pot just for money (the stuff you are probably already using and have been using for a long time) to change their ways in order to compete with the grade of marijuana you can grow yourself. Hopefully, proper medicine will get to all those in need.

# Chapter 1

# Building Your Grow Room

The key to success with any urban indoor garden is the grow room. To achieve high-grade, high-yielding marijuana, your plants must live and grow in a perfect environment. You need to protect your home from molds and pests as well as assuring your personal safety. An odor, light leakage, or loud noise can tip off others about your urban marijuana garden, which could lead to some serious problems. Even if you are a legal marijuana grower, you should treat the situation as though you were growing illegally. If your secret gets out, you might find yourself the victim of a home invasion or, at the very least, discrimination from your neighbors. With the room design tips shown in this book, you should be completely covered. The cost of building your garden this way may seem expensive, but you will earn back your outlay with your first grow – and the safety of yourself and your home is priceless.

## ■ Preparing the floor, ceiling, and walls

The goal in this design is to keep your garden completely contained from the rest of your home, the outside of your home, and most of all, from other people.

### Step 1

First, start with your garden's floor. Glue or staple some cheap, 'nothing special' white or beige vinyl flooring to the floor. Another option is to paint the floor with a white, outdoor, weather-protected paint, which is easier and cheaper if you are using a basement cement floor or wood subfloor. Sometimes water spills on the floor and runs through your pot; you want to protect the floor from water damage, and avoid disturbing anything below your garden, if it is not in the basement. Your floor will also need to be easily mopped up and cleaned with bleach.

## Step 2

Completely cover the walls and ceiling inside of your grow room (we will cover the windows and entrance later) with Dura Edge all-weather insulation board. You may have seen this at a new home construction site. Cover the entire inside of the grow room as shown here. You can nail up the insulation board with a roof nail or, to create the minimum damage to be repaired after growing, you can use heavy-duty double-sided carpet tape as well.

## Step 3

Next, start to seal up the grow room. Take some caulking silicone and caulk all the major seams in the room, down at the floor, the ceiling, and all of the corners of the room as shown here. Allow to dry.

## Step 4

After the silicone is dry, take some "tuck tape" (sheathing tape not duct tape) and cover all of the seams between the pieces of insulation. Do the same to the ceiling as well. This will prevent any chance of mold being spread to the rest of your house

or apartment and will be a major factor in odor control too. In addition, this will help prevent pests entering the grow room.

## Step 5

Take a roll of black and white plastic. You can find this at your local grow store. With the white side of the plastic facing the inside of the room, tape it up with double-sided carpet tape. Now you have a nice bright white grow room, which will facilitate reflection of light, increasing the garden's production. It can also be cleaned with bleach, which should be done after every grow, and will act as a vapour seal for the insulation.

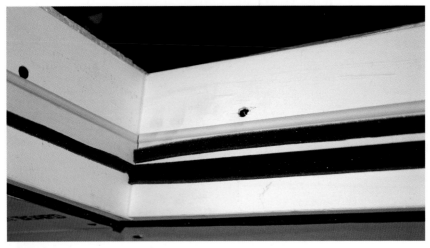

## Step 6

For your entrance, you want the same type of setup as you have with the front door to your home. Seal the door completely with weather stripping, including the floor, to ensure a tight fit. You don't want any odor or light to escape. An even better option (which is not always possible) is to create a false or secret door. I will discuss this later in the book.

## ■ One-light garden setup

A single-light setup is very simple and cheap, but still highly effective. If you don't have the space for a multiple-light garden, or if you just want to keep it small, simple and cheap, then the one-light setup is for you. You will need a room that can hold at least a 4- x 5.5-foot growing space. By "growing space", we just mean the amount of space in which actual plant matter will be growing. You will also need two clean 15-amp electrical circuits in the room. When I say "clean circuit," I mean there must be nothing else plugged in or running on those two circuits. They are for your garden's use only. You will need the following equipment:

- ■ 1 x 1,000-watt High Intensity Discharge (HID) Ballast
- ■ 1 x heavy-duty timer
- ■ 1 x High Pressure Sodium (HPS) bulb
- ■ 1 x shade

No matter how many plants you are growing, I would never suggest having any less than one 1,000-watt light. You can use the instructions in this book if you choose to grow with a smaller light, but do not expect the same results whatsoever. The heavy-duty timer will need to be installed on one of your clean circuits; please hire a professional electrician to do this. Next, we need equipment to keep the room temperature controlled and to maintain good airflow for the garden. You will need one four-inch exhaust fan to exhaust heat coming from the 1,000-watt light, an oscillating

## ■ Equipment you will need for your one-light setup

*High Intensity Discharge (HID) Ballast.*

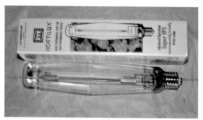

*High Pressure Sodium (HPS) bulb.*

*Heavy duty timer.*

*Four-inch exhaust fan.*

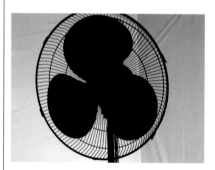

Oscillating fan.

*Squirrel cage fan.*

*Temperature and humidity thermostat.*

*Four-inch charcoal filter.*

fan for good airflow, and a small squirrel cage fan to suck new air into the room. A temperature and humidity thermostat will be required as well. The thermostat should be able to tell you when your humidity or temperature is too high or too low. Check these measurements every day. We will go more in depth with this later in the book. Finally, for odor control we will need a four-inch charcoal filter for the exhaust fan, which will scrub the air in your garden and push clean air out, preventing the neighborhood from getting a constant whiff of your cannabis.

### Step 1

To begin setting up your one-light garden, mark out your 4- x 5.5-foot growing space on the ceiling.

### Step 2

Build support for the lights. Measure the length of the shade, then screw in two 2x4s using deck screws in the ceiling, centered in your growing space to the stud on your ceiling.

### Step 3

Use ceiling hooks and chains to hang the lights. I don't advise leaving the ballast on the floor in case you spill some water, so put it up on a table or shelf for safety. This ballast is to be plugged into the circuit with the timer all by itself. That will be a 15-amp circuit and the 1,000-watt light is going to draw a good constant of 11 amps. Do not attempt to plug anything else in to this circuit, or you risk causing an electrical fire.

## Step 4

If there is a window in the room, use it to exhaust the heat from your garden. If a window is not available, exhaust the heat into another part of the house - preferably above the garden, since heat rises. Do not worry about odor, as we are going to attach that four-inch charcoal filter to scrub the air clean. You should hang the fan up high in your room with ceiling hooks and bungee cords; all the hot air will rise to the top of your room and the bungee cords reduce the vibrations and noise caused by the fan, keeping your garden quiet. Plug that four-inch exhaust fan and your oscillating fan in to the remaining clean circuit. I will show you how to use the oscillating fan later in the book.

## Step 5

Finally, we take the thermostat and hang it mid level on any wall in the room. If your entrance is sealed when closed, use a squirrel cage fan to suck new air into your garden

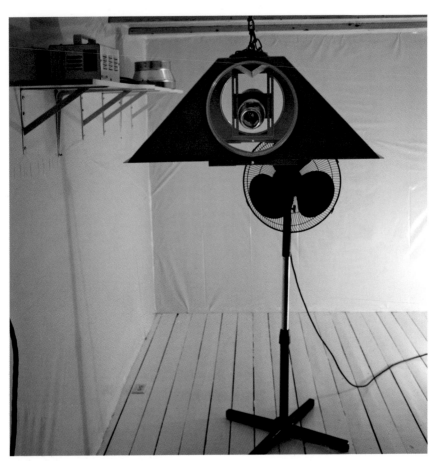

(intake). Simply place it close to the floor and have it suck in air from another room in the house or apartment. Do not have it suck air straight from outdoors. You will learn how to use all this equipment more thoroughly over the course of this book.

## ■ Two-light garden setup

For the two-light setup you will need a room that can hold a growing space of 4- x 8.5-feet, plus you will need at least 3 clean circuits in the room as well. The following lighting equipment will be needed:

- 2 x 1,000-watt HID ballasts
- 2 x air-cooled shades
- 2 x 1,000-watt HPS bulbs
- 1 x eight-inch exhaust fan

An air-cooled shade is an enclosure over the bulb with glass, allowing it to let an exhaust fan suck the heat of the bulb to outside of your garden directly. You will need ceiling hooks and chain to hang the shades and maybe some shelving for the ballasts. To suck out the heat from the lights, you will need an eight-inch 750 CFM or higher exhaust fan with some eight-inch flex duct, and an eight-inch charcoal filter to scrub the air being sucked out of the garden. You'll also need at least one oscillating fan for airflow. You will need to install a four-inch exhaust fan for an intake in this setup. Finally, you will need a high and low reading thermostat and humidistat.

The CFM rating for the exhaust fan stands for Cubic Feet per Minute. This is a reading used to measure the air volume velocity of the fan. For this two-light setup for example, we are exhausting two light shades and a charcoal filter. Each shade will need 200 CFM and the filter will need 200 CFM as well. This means that we will need a minimum of 600 CFM exhaust power for proper operating results.

---

■ **Equipment you will need for your two-light setup**

*Two 1,000-watt HID ballasts.*

*Two 1,000-watt HPS bulbs and shades.*

*Eight-inch 750 CFM or higher exhaust fan.*

*Eight-inch flex duct.*

*Eight-inch charcoal filter.*

*Four-inch exhaust fan.*

## Step 1

We will start off hanging the light shades first. Mark out on the ceiling your 4- x 8.5-foot growing space. Your shades should have two hooks each for hanging. Measure this distance for the width of the placement for the ceiling hooks. Next measure 4.5 feet in between, to place the hooks for the second shade. Center that in your growing space, and put your support beams on the ceiling to screw in your hooks.

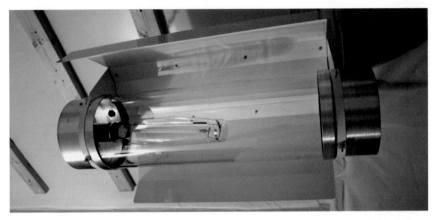

## Step 2

Hang the chain and lights, and then screw in your light bulbs, as shown in the picture.

## Step 3

Next we are going to turn the exhaust fan, the two lights and the charcoal filter into one big exhaust line.

Take the eight-inch exhaust fan and hang it up with the bungee cords, so it will blow the air out towards the outtake of the room. Line up the fan three feet in front of your first light.

## Step 4

Attach the eight-inch duct from the back of the exhaust fan towards your window or to another room in your home. Use duct tape or tuck tape to attach to the fan first, then add a metal clamp for extra security.

## Step 5

Now attach the duct using duct tape or your tuck tape from the front of the exhaust fan to the front of the first light.

## Step 6

From the other side of the first light, run duct to the second light beside it. The second light bulb must point in the direction of the exhaust fan.

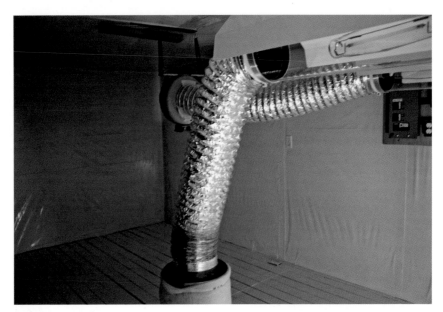

## Step 7

Take your eight-inch charcoal filter, and place it on the floor at the end of the second light beside the exhaust fan, then attach your duct from the filter to the second light. Now we have created one big exhaust line, taking the smelly air and heat through the charcoal filter, and exhausting clean hot air out of the room. When you're taping the connections make sure they are completely sealed and tight for best performance.

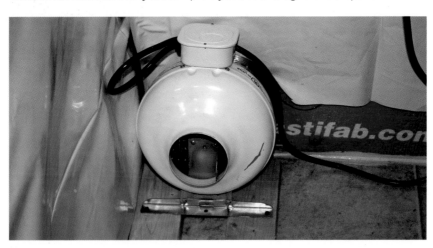

## Step 8

Next, set up a four-inch exhaust fan or a squirrel cage fan near the floor anywhere in the room. This should suck air from another room into the garden; do not suck the air from outside.

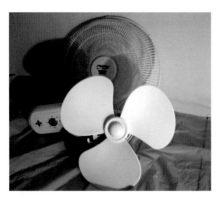

## Step 9

Place your thermostat two thirds of the way up any wall in the room so it can obtain a fairly accurate overall reading. If you do not have the space for an oscillating fan, you can get a wall-mounted one to save room.

## Step 10

Plug each light into your professionally installed heavy-duty timer(s) and all remaining fans into the third clean circuit.

■ **Equipment you will need for your four or six-light setup**

Ten-inch 1,050 CFM or higher exhaust fan.    Small portable a/c unit.

Ten-inch to eight-inch reducer.    Ten-inch insulated duct.

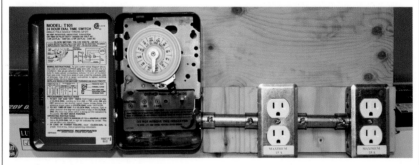

240-watt circuit board.

## ■ Four- and six-light setup

The two- and four-light gardens are very similar. Just as we did in the two-light garden, we want to create one big exhaust line, removing both heat and odor. This is vital for a perfect environment in your urban garden. For the four-light garden you will need the following equipment:

- 1 x ten-inch 1,050 CFM or higher exhaust fan
- 1 x eight-inch charcoal filter for odor control
- 1 x ten-inch to eight-inch reducer
- 2 x bungee cords to hang the fan
- 4 x eight-inch air cooled shades with 1,000-watt HPS bulbs and HID ballasts
- 1 x eight-inch Y duct piece for ducting
- 1 x eight-inch flex duct
- 1 x ten-inch insulated duct

We use insulated duct to significantly reduce air noise coming out of the room. You could get some eight-inch insulated duct for the back of your exhaust fan for the two-light setup as well, if you feel it's necessary. Also, you will need at least two oscillating fans, and a thermostat with humidity monitoring. Have your electrician run a 240-watt circuit into the room, then purchase a four-light electrical board with a timer, which you can buy at your local grow store. The board will plug in to the 240-watt circuit. Just as in the two-light setup, we are going to create one big exhaust line using your shades and fan.

### Step 1

First, measure your growing area out on the ceiling, so you can place the lights in the best spot for light spectrum. You will need a 7.5- x 8.5-foot growing space, placing your lights parallel to each other in pairs. You should use a ten-inch exhaust fan to suck out the heat, and cap the line with an eight-inch charcoal filter. These two lines of lights should be about 1.5 feet apart in the middle, and the lights should be 1.5 feet in front of each other. This will give you a fuller light spectrum, and a more extensive prime light area over your garden, leading to a higher overall yield.

## Step 2

Use 2x4s to support the lights and give you good positioning for your room size, then hang the lights with hooks and chains and screw in your 1,000-watt HPS bulbs.

## Step 3

Hang up the ten-inch exhaust fan with the bungee cords to reduce noise and vibra-tion. Leave a good 3 to 4 feet between the fans and your lights so you can move the lights up and down later while growing.

 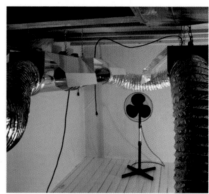

## Step 4

Attach the ten- to eight-inch reducer to the front of the ten-inch fan. Now you can attach the duct from the exhaust fan to the lights to the charcoal filter on the end, creating one exhaust line as shown. Again, do not worry about odor since we are using charcoal filters on the exhaust line to eliminate all smells. Remember when hanging your exhaust fans that the air should be blowing out towards the window or exhausting room. Place your oscillating fans wherever you feel is best for airflow.

## Step 5

I suggest you use a four-inch exhaust fan of 200 CFM or higher for a fresh air intake. Place it low to the ground and have it suck air from another part of your house or apartment. Make sure you are not sucking air straight from the outside, since that may bring unwanted elements in to the garden.

## Step 6

Finally, hang your high- and low-reading thermostat two thirds of the way up on any wall in the room for the best overall reading. Later in the book, we will take a look at disguising vents at a window or in another room of your home. Here is a finished 4-light setup.

## ■ Equipment you will need for your four or six-light setup

*Eight-inch Y-duct connector.*

*Eight-inch charcoal filters.*

*A single line out of the room, behind fans.*

*Ten-inch to eight-inch reducer.*

*Inline fan setup.*

*Six light electrical board with timer.*

*Y-Duct connector setup.*

For the four-light setup, you will need this equipment in addition to the equipment listed above:

- 2 x 1,000-watt HID light sets
- 1 x eight-inch charcoal filter
- 1 x eight-inch exhaust fan
- 1 x eight-inch Y-duct connector

In this design, there will be two rows of three lights running parallel to each other. Both lines will be capped with eight-inch charcoal filters. The eight-inch Y-connector is to be attached to the front of the exhaust fans, allowing you to use a single line out behind the fans out of the room. When attaching the Y-connector to the front of the eight-inch exhaust fan, first tape it and then add a metal clamp. When choosing an 8-inch exhaust fan, make sure the CFM is higher than 700 to give you more exhaust power. Place the eight-inch fan in line, in front of the ten-inch fan, using the ten-inch to eight-inch reducer to connect them. This will give you sufficient CFM for the setup. Your intake, oscillating fans, and thermostat remain the same as the 4-light setup. Your growing area will increase to 11 x 8 feet. Buy a six-light electrical board with timer that will plug into a 240-watt circuit. Please hire a professional electrician; do not attempt to do the electrical work yourself.

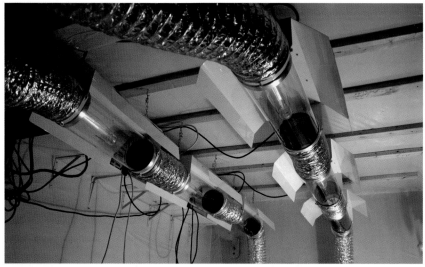

## ■ Airflow

You now have an intake bringing new air to the room and an outtake removing old hot air; leave these fans running at all times. The oscillating fans will push and move the air around the room and your plants. Have these fans at a medium speed, oscillating over the whole garden. The fan leaves on the plants absorb this breeze, making the plant protect itself by resonating harder. A warning: you can have too much of a breeze on the plants, causing windburn, which will hurt the plant and stunt its growth.

## ■ Humidity

Another tip for making the plant protect itself is to keep humidity low. Just to be safe, and to be free of mold and most insects, keep the humidity below 45%. It is impossible for mold to form in your room or on the plants if your humidity is below this level. Depending on where you live and what season it is, you might require the assistance of a dehumidifier to keep this low humidity, especially when the lights are off.

## ■ Temperature

With the lights on, the temperature in your grow room should be around 75° F and with the lights off, around 70°. Depending on your location and the time of year, you might require a portable air conditioning unit just for the garden; simply set the thermostat on the unit and leave it to run. Today, most of these units have a dehumidifier built in, so you can take care of both things at once. If you need to extend the exhaust on one of these units you can add a booster fan to the line. To increase heat in the wintertime, when the lights are off, purchase a space heater with a thermostat. Simply set the temperature and leave.

## ■ Night Lighting

You can install a green flood light in your grow room, which will allow you to see your plants and let you move in your grow room when the lights are turned off. The green light will not affect the photosynthesis process.

## ■ Trouble shooting and unusual situations

One possible but unusual situation that may arise, depending on the space you have to designate for your garden, is not having any windows to exhaust your heat. There are a few solutions to this problem, but the best one is to exhaust the heat to another room in your home, away from your garden and the garden's intake. If you have a garage that you can run your exhaust to, this is perfect, as it gives you a heated garage and is easy to disguise. Another popular solution is to attach your exhaust to your furnace or central air-conditioning unit's exhaust, which will exhaust your heat directly outside and is undetectable from outside of your home.

Some people, depending on where they live, have damp basements. This can be detrimental to your garden and your home, so dehumidifiers will be needed both inside and outside your garden, running at all times. Most dehumidifiers use a bucket to trap the water they have pulled from the air and will shut off when it becomes full. Simply modify a hose to connect to the dehumidifier and run it to your basement drain to prevent the dehumidifier from shutting off. If the humidity goes over seventy percent, your plants and your home will be at risk of mold.

# Chapter 2

# Getting Your Plants Started

## ■ Starting seeds

Normally, seed companies sell seeds in packs of ten, so we will assume you have ten seeds in this lesson. The strain I'm going to use is a Sweet Pink Grapefruit crossed with Nepalese (which is used to make hash). There are many different ways to germinate seeds; germinating means causing the seed to sprout prior to planting. Some people will germinate using rockwool cubes or a cup of water while others germinate their seeds in soil. We will do it the old-school way: using two plates, paper towel, and distilled water.

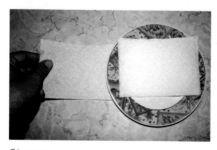

**Step 1**

Get two equal-sized plates, then cut three pieces of paper towel that fit inside your plates.

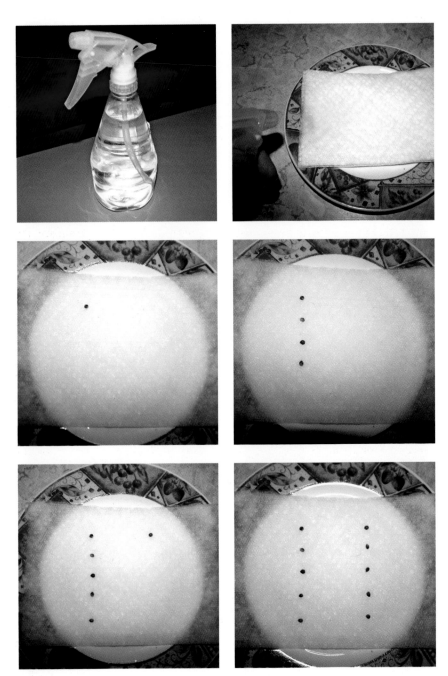

## Step 2

Using a spray bottle, spray distilled water over your paper towel pieces until they are completely moist. Then place your seeds on the moist paper towel, making sure they are at least half an inch to an inch apart from each other.

## Step 3

Cut another three pieces of paper towel as you did in Step One. Place them over the top of your seeds and spray completely with distilled water until totally moist. Basically, we are making a wet seed sandwich with paper towels.

## Step 4

Take your second plate and place it upside down on top of the first plate. This will block out light and trap humidity. Then place it on a heating mat or a warm place in the dark.

### ■ Seeds Starting to Grow

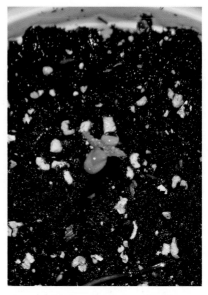

*Germinated seed sprouting for first time. Let the shell fall off naturally.*

*First set of leaves appearing after the shell naturally falls off.*

*After one week the sprout is now good and strong.*

*Make sure you keep your light close to newly growing plants to encourage a strong structure.*

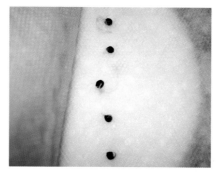

## Step 5

Check daily for sprouted seeds and re-spray with distilled water, keeping your paper towel pieces moist at all times. You must not let them dry out. You could find that your seeds have sprouted anywhere within twenty-four hours to ten days. If ten days go by and nothing sprouts, you either did something wrong or the seeds are duds.

## Step 6

Once your seeds have sprouted, we are going to plant them in a plastic cup with moist soil. First, fill your cup with moist soil and pat it down lightly. Then, take one sprouted seed and stick it gently in the middle of your cup, sprout-end first, with the shell on top. Next, lightly cover the seed with your soil. You want it only about a centimeter deep. If there is too much soil above your seed it will not have the strength to pop out of the soil. Repeat this for all seeds in separate cups.

### Step 7

Place your cup under a fluorescent light. Make sure it is practically touching the cup—the light must be slammed on the plant at all times for the next two weeks. Just slightly raise your light as the sprout just about touches the bulb. If you do not do this, your plant will be extremely stretched and will turn out deformed, with poor structure. When the plant is about four to six inches big, it is ready to be planted in a pot of your choice.

## ■ Sexing

Keep your plants in the vegetative stage until they are twenty-four inches tall, so we can start the process of finding out what sex each plant is. Plants will either be male or female or both (hermaphrodites). To find out what sex each plant is we must make them start to flower. Some growers do this quickly by leaving the plants completely in the dark for three to four days. However, I suggest that you just change your light cycle to twelve hours and give the plants a week to a week and a half to start to turn.

### Males

Once your plants have started to flower you should be able to tell their sex. If a plant is male, when a pistil sprouts it will produce a couple of pods underneath it, just like a penis and testicles. As soon as you see these pods, unless you are going to make a batch of seeds, throw out the plant immediately, or it will pollinate your female plants. Here is a picture of a male two weeks into flower.

## Females

Females are very easy to detect. The flowers that have just started will be all pistils as shown. If you plan to clone your plant, change your light cycle back to eighteen hours within two weeks of flowering the plant. This will flip the plant back into the vegetative state so you can cut clones for a future date. If not, and you're growing all of your plants straight from seed, then just continue to flower them till the end. You're only looking at a 50/50 split between male and female with your seeds, so I do not suggest growing straight from seed. Grow from seed only to give you a new strain—which you can mother and grow over and over again.

## Hermaphrodites

Hermaphrodites are very hard to detect. You normally find them when buying all-feminized seeds, as feminized seeds are not natural. As mentioned above, any batch of seeds will naturally be a mix of both male and female seeds; to make a batch 'feminized' all the seeds are treated with chemicals, forcing the male seeds to turn female. I find this only partially works, and tends to produce hermaphrodites. To detect a hermaphrodite you must check every branch of your twenty-four-inch plant to see if it is male or female. A hermaphrodite will have some branches that are male and some that are female; you must check for both. If some of the branches are male it will have the same effect as a full male by seeding your entire crop. Be careful with feminized seeds; sometimes they are more of a problem than regular seeds.

*A mother garden with a 400watt Metal Halide light. All you need is the light, timer and small oscillating fan.*

## ■ Building a mother garden

Building a mother garden is nowhere near as difficult or extensive as building the gardens shown in chapter one. Your mothers remain in a vegetative state at all times, so your temperature and humidity and odor control are almost non-issues. A mother plant is a plant that is used to give multiple cuts to grow into other plants for each crop. You can cut from a mother for up to a year, but I suggest you start one from scratch for each grow. For a mother garden, all you need is air to come in and out. You can build a room from scratch or simply use a closet with a small squirrel cage fan, or even make a four-inch hole up high in your space to let the air out. The crack underneath the door is all you need for an intake. For mothers, all you will need is a 400-watt MH (Metal Halide) light kit and a small oscillating fan.

Just hang your light, turn on your oscillating fan, and, if you like, line the walls with Black and White plastic for better results. You can use a hardwire timer for this setup or just a simple heavy-duty plug-in timer. Above are pictures of a mother garden setup, just a frame covered in black and white plastic for walls.

*Make sure you leave two new nodes to grow when trimming a mother, and always cut on an angle away from your body.*

## ■ Mother maintenance

To feed your mothers all you use is a vegetative nutrient. Use only 2/3 the recommended dosage on the bottle at all times. As your mothers grow, they will need to be pruned. When you cut a top node, there will be two little nodes underneath, which, since the top has been cut, will grow out into two new cuttings. A node is the part of the plant that sprouts, creating new branches during growth; once the plant has flowered, the nodes will stop appearing and will flower. Continue to prune until your plant has reached the right size for this to take place, roughly once it is over twenty-four inches tall. This will give you a bushier plant, thus giving you plenty of prime cuttings for you to take to your next garden. I find that keeping mothers going for a whole year gets really messy and the plant ends up taking a beating over time, resulting in weaker clones. I start new mothers each grow, taking one out to veg. By the time you need to take cuttings for your next garden, your mother should be large enough to give thirty to forty cuttings, at least enough for a twenty-five plant garden; this book is entirely based on a twenty-five plant garden.

## ■ Cloning Equipment

*Six-inch dome.*

*Seedling heating mat.*

*Bottle of rooting gel (I like to use Wilson's).*

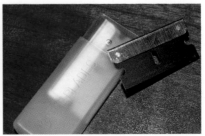

*Razor blade.*

*Nail.*

*Fluorescent light.*

*Bottle of distilled water.*

*Flat of rockwool cubes.*

# Cloning: setting up your station and making clones

Cloning is when we take a cutting from a mother and try to make it root as a new plant. For many growers out there, cloning is a very difficult thing to succeed at, and there are many different theories that people have on how to do so. I'm going to give you the same lesson that was originally given to me, which I have had great success with for many years. You will need the following:

- 1 six-inch dome
- 1 seedling heating mat
- 1 bottle of rooting gel
  (I like to use Wilson's)
- 1 razor blade
- 1 nail
- 1 fluorescent light
- 1 spray bottle with distilled water
- 1 flat of Rockwool cubes

## Step 1

First we must pH-balance our rockwool cubes. You can use a special agent to do this or go the old fashioned route, which is to soak the cubes in plain water for at least twenty-four hours to balance them out naturally. Break two pieces from your rockwool flat: four rows of seven cubes each. Place them in a fifteen-liter bucket of hot water and soak for twenty-four hours.

## Step 2

Now that our rockwool cubes are pH-balanced, we add 1/3 of our vegetative nutrient's recommended dosage and let the cubes soak for another ten to fifteen minutes, to let the nutrients get inside the cubes.

## Step 3

In order for our clones to root we must allow some oxygen flow through the rockwool cubes, so we must drain out all of the loose water soaking in the cubes. Taking one piece at a time, grip both sides of the piece and shake the excess water out into a bucket. You can tell when it's finished by judging the color and weight of the rockwool cubes. When the water is almost gone, it will go from dark to a light yellow and your rockwool will be less than half the weight it was before shaking out the water.

## Step 4

Place both pieces on the tray of your dome. For the next step, we must resize the holes in the rockwool cubes to fit our cuttings. Take a regular-sized nail and size it up to your rockwool cube, leaving about half an inch up from the table, and then grip the nail with two fingers on the top of the rockwool cubes. Stick the nail down every single hole, using your grip to the nail as a measurement for how deep the holes will be.

## Step 5

Using a sharp razor, take a cutting from your mother, making sure to cut it on an angle. This will give more surface space for a root ball to start. We want at least one inch of

bare stalk to go in the cube, so most likely you will have to cut off one or two leaves with your blade. When finished, stick the trimmed cutting in the bottle of rooting gel.

## Step 6

Gently take the dipped cutting and place it in one of your newly made holes until it reaches the bottom of the hole in the rockwool cube. Do not force it in; you want it to be snug but not tight. If you have trouble fitting it in then pull it out, re-dip the cutting, take your nail, and stick it in the hole to make a better size to fit for your cutting. Every strain will have a different size of stalk. Repeat this step until you have cut twenty clones for each four-by-seven set of rockwool cubes.

## ■ Cloning maintenance

Once you are finished making your clones, put on the dome lid and place the dome on a seedling heating mat under a fluorescent light. Place an object of your choice on the heating mat to raise the dome a half an inch to an inch off the mat. Placing the dome directly on the mat will give you a little too much heat for the dome, so I like to adjust it a bit. Make six holes with a nail in the lid of the dome for ventilation, one in every corner and two in the middle. Have your fluorescent light almost touching the lid of the dome; you want to give them as much light as possible. Leave the light on twenty-four hours a day through this entire process. Every day after you wake up and before you go to bed, take the lid off the dome for thirty minutes to let them get some air. When you first take off the lid, spray vigorously with your bottle of distilled water all over your cuttings; this will be dry before the half hour is up. After spraying, leave the dome back under the lights with the lid off for the

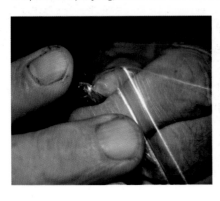 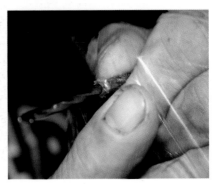

entire thirty minutes, and then put the lid back on. If you can do this a third time in the middle of your day as well, that would be better, but it's not entirely necessary.

In about fourteen days, your cuttings should have mostly rooted and will need to be fed again. If they are not all finished, continue until they are all done. They will need to be fed at least once; to do this, pour one quart from your cloning feed slowly into one side of the tray and then pour another quart at the other end of the tray. Give it ten minutes to soak up the feed then put the lid back on and place the dome back under your fluorescent light.

## ■ Rooted Clones

*Take lid off the dome and gently lift bottom of rockwool cubes to see if you have roots.*

*Take your time and be gentle when pulling rooted cuttings apart.*

MARIJUANA MADE SIMPLE: A BEGINNER'S GUIDE TO GROWING LIKE A PRO

*Cup rooted cuttings in beer cups, filling the cup with moist soil first, then gently plant.*

## ■ Cupping Clones

Once you have enough cuttings rooted and ready to be planted, you will want to start them in beer cups or red party cups full of soil, with two nail holes punched in the bottom of each cup for drainage. Place them under a fluorescent light, with the light on 24 hours a day, for at least a week. This will give time for the roots to catch to the dirt, so they can start to grow. After the week is finished your plants will be strong enough to go under the 1,000-watt light/s, and will take right off. If you place your freshly rooted cuttings directly into the main garden, they will spend a week just getting over the stress, and you will be paying to run your 1,000 watt light/s for nothing.

# ■ pH and nutrient levels

pH is a measurement of the acidity or alkalinity of a solution. When we make up a nutrient solution to feed the plants, we must make sure that the acidity level is not too high or low or we will cause damage to our plants. Some take this very seriously; they believe that certain pH levels make an enormously positive influence on your plants. Most people say that for hydro gardens the ultimate pH level is 6.0, and for soil gardens it is 7.0. I have tried everything and never noticed a difference with the

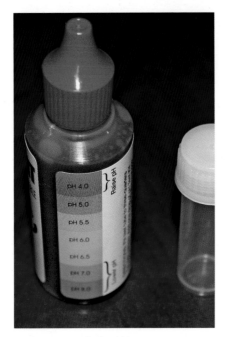

*Basic PH test solution kit.*

outcome of my plants. For this growing system, just make sure (after you have added all of your nutrients) to check that your pH level is within 5.5 and 7.5. If necessary, add a pH-up or pH-down solution to get in within that range. You only need to check this every time you have added something new or made a change with your nutrient mixture. To check the levels, just use a basic Iodine solution pH testing kit and follow the directions.

The same thing goes with checking your EC level (measurement of nutrients) in regards to this growing system; checking the EC level is only necessary for people who are obsessed with the weight of their crop, who overfeed using more than maximum dosages throughout their growing cycle hoping to get a greater yield. This is cheating and leaves you with very dirty medicine, which is not acceptable for every day medical use. The way I teach you to feed the plants leaves you in no danger of having high EC levels and still leaves you with a good yield.

# ■ Soil mixtures, potting, and planting

There are many different soil companies out there; the one I use is called Pro Mix. For this growing style you need to add perlite to your soil. Perlite helps to keep moisture in your soil for longer. I also like to add worm castings to my soil mixture, as it is a great organic fertilizer.

If you do not use perlite in your soil mixture, the plants will dry out almost twice as fast, and will not match feeding schedules in chapter 6. I strongly recommend investing in a bag, as the rewards will be well worth it.

## Step 1

Take a large Rubbermaid container and fill it up with half a bale of potting soil. Break up all hard pieces and make it nice and loose.

## Step 2

If you do not already have perlite in your soil mix, fill up a seven-gallon pot and mix it in with the soil in the Rubbermaid container.

Add fifteen liters of worm castings, and mix in with the soil.

### Step 3

Add fifteen liters of plain water to the top of your soil mixture; we want to moisten the soil in layers—only moisten a foot of your soil at a time. You can start planting after each layer of soil is moistened.

### Step 4

Scoop up the soil with both hands and lightly drop it into each pot until full. Leave a couple of inches from the top to make it easier to feed later.

## Step 5

Take two fingers and make a hole in the center of your soil.

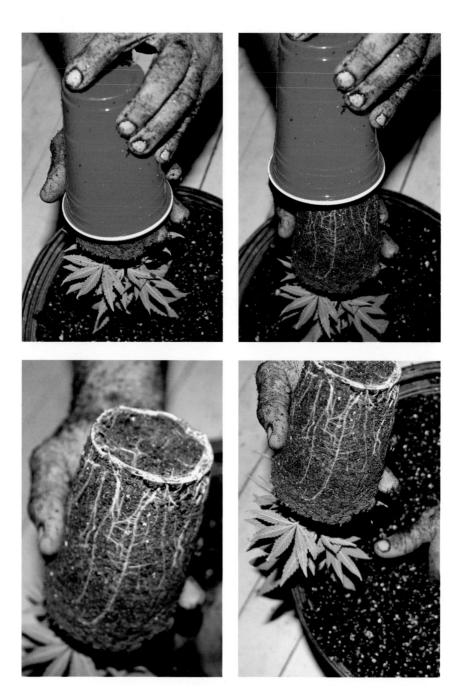

Place your rooted clone or cupped plant gently into the hole and cover over with the soil. With one hand, gently level the top of your soil while patting it down at the same time. Remember, just like the rockwool cubes with the cloning, we want some oxygen to get inside the soil, so do not pack your pots too tight.

Now you're finally ready to start growing!

# Chapter 3

# The Vegetative Cycle

## ■ What is vegetative growth?

Now that you are finished with cloning and potting, you can begin the production of the new plants. The first stage is the vegetative cycle. Outdoors, during the spring, all plants are in their vegetative state. During this process the plants will grow at a good rate, setting up their structure for the year so they can start to

bloom. You will do the same thing, but indoors. The only difference is that with your high-powered lighting system, high-end nutrients, and controlled environment, the process will take two to three weeks, instead of two to three months.

## ■ Light cycle

Your plants know what growth phase they are in based on the light cycle. In the spring we receive more daylight than in the winter or the fall, and this extra daylight tells the plants to grow. Indoors, to create a fake spring lighting cycle, have the lights on the plants for a longer period: 18 hours a day is the recommended time. If you like, you can leave the lights on for 24 hours a day, but this does not have any effect on the process and is a waste of resources. You will find that once the plants get bigger after fourteen to fifteen hours of light time they will start to go limp, getting ready for bedtime. 18 hours a day is the absolute minimum, however; don't try to save money by only having your lights on 15 or 16 hours a day. I have tried everything, and you will need a minimum of 18 hours a day to do the trick.

## ■ Preparing the garden

The first thing to do is to clean the garden. Take bleach and hot water and wash the floors, walls, and ceiling thoroughly. Now to set up your equipment: if you are going with a one-light, two-light, or four-light garden, then set your timer to be on for 18 hours a day. There are two schools of thought as to whether it is better to run your 'daylight' 18-hours-on cycle in the daytime or the night; I suggest that you run your 'daytime' cycle at night, as you can avoid peak electricity usage hours, costing you significantly less in the long run. Also, it is cooler at night, making it easier to run and control the equipment in your garden, which saves you money and extends the life of your equipment. If you are going with a six-light garden, then all you need to use is one row of three lights for this stage, with a timer set to 18 hours on. Use one oscillating fan to blow air over the entire growing space and leave your exhaust fan on, along with the oscillating fan, for 24 hours a day. For this stage you don't need to use charcoal filters as there should be no issue with odor at this stage. However, each grow room is different, so if you feel there is an odor issue then by all means hook them up.

Ideally you want to maintain a temperature of 73–75° F in the garden when the lights are on, and 70–73° F when the lights are off. It is okay to have higher temperatures, as long as you do not go over the low 80s. Once temperature exceeds this point, the plants will become stressed, which will have an effect on your final yield. The temperature must not fluctuate more than 15 degrees between

the lights-on and light-off periods, as this can give rise to various problems, such as powdery mildew, and if you have bugs this will help the infestation grow worse. Depending on how many lights you are running you might require an air conditioning unit in the summer and a space heater in the winter in order to keep ideal conditions. Just set the desired temperature on either the air conditioner or heater and leave.

For humidity, lower is better. This will eliminate any chance of mold in your garden, as well as increasing resin accumulation on your bud. For best results, keep the humidity under 50%. If it's above 65–70%, you will require a dehumidifier. Remember the temperature and humidity of your grow room must be checked daily, both when lights are off and on. Finally, attach a rubber garden hose to the nearest water tap so you can fill up your fifteen-liter bucket to feed the plants.

## ■ Pot and light placement

When growing, make the most of your lights at all times. To do this, consider the placement of the plants under the lights; you will be able to fit nine plants under each light at this stage. Simply place them centered under your light in rows of three. For vegetative growth using the six-light setup, you will only use the one row of three lights as shown. Now consider light decapitation. For the first day of veg, keep the lights up high, at least four feet above the top of your plants. Do this for the first day to allow your little babies to adjust to the 1,000-watt lights they have just been placed under. For day two, drop the lights to two feet above the top of your plants. I will tell you when they will need to be raised next throughout the chapter. You want to make the plants grow into the light but not take any shock from the lights since they are very small and can be easily damaged or stressed out. By the time they reach the light they will be bigger and stronger, allowing them to take more light power without damage.

Unless you are a master grower, not all of your plants will be the same size. To make all of your plants eventually even, increase the amount of light the smaller ones receive. Each light has a hot spot, normally in the middle of the shade, so keep the larger plants on the outside rows of the lights and the smaller ones in the middle. Also, raise the smaller plants: you can use a piece of wood or anything else of your choice for this. I like to use leftover cigar boxes for this myself. This will give them more light decapitation than the rest of the plants, making them grow faster so they can catch up to the others. Once the smaller plants have caught up in size, drop them back down to the same level as the rest of the plants. Don't worry if you are confused at this stage; I will show you every step throughout the rest of the chapter.

# ■ Week one—structure and feeding

### Day One

For this grow, we are going to use a twenty-five plant setup under six lights, as this is a fairly common size for someone with a medical license. The strain we will be using is called Blastaberry, a Strawberry Diesel (Strawberry Cough x NYC Diesel) x Indica Blueberry cross. I chose the Blastaberry because it has a very common flower structure, but is very difficult to grow due to its thin stalk and heavy bud. I will show you the structure of a short bush-style plant at the end of this chapter.

Place your plants in three rows of eight, centered under one row of three lights. Take the last plant and place it centered in front of your three rows. Your 25th plant should always be your smallest, weakest plant. We will use this plant as a mother for the next grow. Since you have at least a couple of months to veg the plant, we choose a small plant that has time to catch up. For day one the lights should be about four feet above the plants to allow them to adjust to the high-powered lighting system.

Now it is time to feed the plants for the first time. Since the plants are smaller and your potting soil is moist from the potting procedure, give them a light feed to start with. Use only one quart and gently pour it in a six- to eight-inch radius around the plant, making sure the rockwool cube gets re-soaked. It is important to keep the cube moist for the first few days until the roots have caught in their new soil environment. With nutrients, only use 30% of the bottle's recommended maximum dosage, since the plants are still too young to take a full dose. After feeding, pull out and clean any leaves that may have been sucked in to the dirt from your feeding, and smooth out the soil, re-securing your freshly planted clone. Do this every time you feed for at least the first week of the vegetative stage.

## Day Two

All you need to do on day two is to drop the lights to two feet above your plants. Now the plants have had a day to adjust to the lights, you can add a little light power, allowing the plants to get stronger before coming closer to the lights. You also should check to see if any of the plants have dried up in the center; if so, repeat your feeding steps from day one to each of the dried out plants.

## Day Three

As shown, at this point your pots should be drying out, some more than others. For early veg, you want to keep them moist, so feed them all once again following the same instructions as day one's feeding, except this time when you pour in your nutrients with one full quart, cover the entire top of the pot. The roots should be spreading to the sides of the pot by now, so it's necessary to keep moisture throughout the entire pot.

## Day Six

Now you should have seen some definite results, and should start to see the plants' structure develop. Still, leave the lights where they are to allow the plants to grow into the lights. On this day, another feeding is required, but this time since the plants are bigger and stronger, increase the feedings to two full quarts each, and use 60% of the maximum dosage given on your nutrient bottle. Remember when pouring to cover the entire top of the soil in the pot with each scoop. You are almost at the halfway point of the vegetative process, and your plants are now a few inches away from being a foot tall. At two feet tall they will be moved out of the vegetative stage.

## ■ Week two—structure and feeding

### Day Ten

The plants should now be well over a foot tall, with more branches giving them a more bushy look. Raise the lights back to two feet above the tops of the plants, repeating the same process as last week and allowing the plants to grow in to the lights. The plants need to be fed again, using the same instructions as day six: two full quarts with 60% of the maximum recommended dosage on the veg nutrient bottle.

### Day Thirteen

The plants should now be about 1.6 feet tall, and very close to the end of the vegetative stage. Feed them once more using the previous feeding instructions. At this point, you can see the plant really taking its shape and becoming bushier and taller. Start measuring the plants daily so you can start the flowering stage on time. Don't forget to do your daily temperature, humidity and equipment checks.

## ■ Finishing your vegetative cycle

### Day 16

Most of the plants will be twenty-four inches tall, and the rest around twenty-two inches, also in need of another feeding. Now that the plants are fully mature in the veg stage they can withstand a full dose of the recommended dosage of the nutrients call and three full quarts of food. Bump up the amount of food since the plants are bigger and feed more; this helps you keep to a one day on/two day off feeding schedule. This will be our last feeding for this cycle.

### Day 17

Our goal is finally met: all of the plants are twenty-four inches tall, and nice and even as well. Now we are ready for the next cycle, which is the flowering cycle. For the first two to three weeks of flowering you won't notice much difference in your plants, but rest assured, you are off to a great start. Here are pictures of the final product.

## ■ Short Bush Structure

A short, bushy structured plant grows outwards, more than up. Veg these type of plants until they're 18 to 20 inches tall, then flip them into flowering. Don't be afraid of ending up with a smaller yield. This is a picture of Red Devil, winner of the 6th annual Toronto Cannabis Cup, at 20 inches and ready to be flipped into flower. It not only won me a cup, but it is one of my best producers as well.

# Chapter 4

# Flower Cycle

## ■ What is flowering?

The flowering stage comes after the vegetative stage, and it is in this stage that the plant gives us our final product. This is a much longer process than the vegetative cycle. Most strains take an average of eight to nine weeks to flower, but there are many strains that take longer than that. For example, I had a strain called Super Silver Haze; it was 13 weeks into flower and still not ready. It's important to do as much research on the strain as possible before you start growing; look it up on the internet or get feedback from other growers or the person who gave you the strain. This way, you have an idea of what to expect. I have also had strains that took less than eight weeks to flower, such as Willy's Wonder, which only takes six weeks. In this chapter I will take you through the whole process and show you a rough way of deciding when your bud will be finished. We will use the most common eight-week flowering cycle with our 24 plants (remember we took out one of the plants to mother for the next round) under six 1,000 watt HPS lights.

To force the plants to flower, change the light cycle. In the vegetative cycle the lights were on for 18 hours a day to mimic springtime indoors. Now we will change that light cycle to 12 hours a day, to mimic fall indoors. Keep the garden climate the same: a cool 75° F when the lights are on and no less than 70° F when the lights are off. The humidity should always be under 50% but if it goes up to 60 to 65% this is ok. The same thing goes for room temperature: Ideally you want a steady 75°F for best results, but your garden can go up to 85°F. Once your garden's temperature exceeds 85°F then you will start to receive substantial heat stress, which will seriously affect your final outcome, and potentially ruin your crop.

*To begin flower stage for a six light setup we spread our plants under all six lights.*

## ■ Pot placement and preparing your plants to flower

For a one- to four-light garden, there should be six plants per light in seven-gallon pots. Center the six plants underneath each light. For the six-light gardens, we want to use only four plants per light, since we have a larger growing space than the others. Here we are trying to fill every inch of available light with bud. As you will see in this chapter, the plants will grow out to all the available square footage of light. Now we will spread out the plants, keeping them centered from three lights to six lights. You should also change the lights' timer to a twelve-hour light cycle. As I mentioned in chapter three, running your lights at night is the most efficient in terms of power consumption and keeping the climate controlled. Keep all types of fans running 24 hours a day.

*Bamboo sticks.*

*Tomato cage.*

Late in the flower cycle, the plants are likely to topple over. To prevent this, use tomato cages and bamboo sticks, which you can find at any garden center. Put the tomato cages on at the beginning of the flowering cycle or you will not be able to get them on later. For the six-light gardens the plants will be too big for a standard tomato cage, so unless you can find a specialty cage big enough, use only the bamboo sticks and use them much later in the flowering cycle. Now you are ready for your plants to begin producing bud to their full potential.

*Flower day one.*

*Flower day four.*

## ■ Weeks one and two—structure and feeding

Weeks one and two are very similar to the vegetative cycle and it will take close to two weeks for the plants to flip into flowering. During this time the plants will continue to grow bigger, as if they were still in veg, until around week four of flowering. By that time the plants should be at least twice the size they are in week 1 of flowering; however, that will be determined by the traits of the particular strain you are growing. For feeding during this time, start with only the flower nutrients. Since the plants are strong and healthy, go straight to the full recommended dosage given, still on a one day on/two days off schedule. This is to give the plants time to use all of the nutrients given to them. Growers that are only concerned with the weight of their final yield will continue to feed the plants even if the pots are still moist; they think that the more they feed the plants, the bigger they will get. This method can cause many problems, such as root and stem disease. Also, when feeding plants so much you have to be very concerned about elevated pH and nutrients levels, which will have a big effect on your plants and can cause damage. By doing

*Flower day seven.*

*Flowers starting to bloom.*

*Flower day thirteen.*

it my way, there is no concern for any of that, and you will get the same if not better results with weight by using less nutrients, saving you time and money. By using less nutrients you will also end up with cleaner and purer plants, giving full flavor and a justified sense of accomplishment.

In this stage, keep the lights close to the plants; within six to 12 inches. You will have to move the lights up almost daily, until week four when the plants stop growing in height. As you will see in the following pictures, on day ten little pistils will be shooting out of the plants, telling you that flowering mode has now begun.

## ■ Weeks three and four—structure and feeding

In weeks three and four continue to use a full dose of flower nutrient, feeding each plant a full three quarts. If you are interested in using a "pre-ripe," which helps promote more flowers to sprout, start using it now; simply follow the recommended dosage on the bottle. Make sure to put the flower nutrient in your bucket of feed first, stir well and then add the pre-ripe and stir well again. You will use the pre-ripe until about the fourth week of flowering. After three weeks of flowering, the plants will start to dry out a day earlier. Once this happens you will have to feed every other day. Keep the lights close to the plants, and check daily to see if they have to be raised to prevent any light damage. Make a path down the middle of your garden, giving you enough space to get in and hand feed each plant. When feeding is finished, slide the plants back to their normal position. Little buds will start to fill in the gaps on the stalk by day 26.

Making a row for feeding.

Flower day sixteen.

Flower day twenty-two.

Flower day twenty-six.

*Flower day twenty-two.*

*Flower day twenty-six.*

*Flower day thirty.*

*Flower day thirty-six.*

## ■ Weeks five to seven—structure and feeding

After week four, the structure of the plants is complete and they will stop growing to concentrate on flowering. Set the lights in their final position, six to eight inches above the plants. Now that there is bud to ripen, you can use a ripening formula with the flower nutrient. This will make the existing bud grow and harden over the next three weeks. At week five, add the full dosage of flower nutrient then add half the recommended dosage of the flower ripening formula of your choice. Feed the plants this mixture in week five only.

For weeks six and seven use a full dosage of the flower nutrient and a full dosage of the ripening formula for both weeks. By week six you should be checking the density of your bud every few days by gently squeezing a flower; the bud should be getting harder. Also, in week six fan leaves should begin to turn a yellowish color. This means that the plants are maturing and the bud is big enough to be eating the nitrogen out of the fan leaves – this isn't exactly good news for the fan leaves, but it is what a grower wants to see. The nitrogen in the leaves gives them the color green; when the nitrogen gets eaten, the leaves turn to yellow. This doesn't look pretty, but by week seven if your plants are toppling over with lots of yellow and dead leaves, do not worry, that is considered to be a good thing.

I'll repeat that: the plants should be almost falling over at this point. Using bamboo sticks, try to prop them back up as best as you can. I don't suggest using more than three bamboo sticks per plant or you will just make a bigger mess – the goal is to give them extra support, not to make it difficult for yourself come harvest time. Wear a long-sleeved shirt while doing this, or you'll find yourself desperately shaving your arms afterwards to get rid of all the resin!

Here are pictures of the plants, weeks five through seven.

*Flower day forty.*

*Nitrogen leaving fan leaves.*

*Flower day forty-four.*

*Flower day forty-eight.*

*This shot helps you gauge when your plants are ready for the final growing stage (leaching).*

*Here is our crop on its final day of leaching, flower day fifty-six.*

## ■ Knowing when the plants are ready to be finished

There are many ways to tell when the plants are ready to be finished. Most growers use a magnifying glass to check that the pistils of the flower have turned to an amber red color, and are very scientific about it. I like to judge by the hardness and density of the bud. Your plants will be ready for the final stage once they have hard buds and half of the dark amber pistils. If, after week seven, this is not evident, you will have to continue feeding them until it is; the buds must be tough and the pistils must be red before your plants can enter the final phase.

## ■ Flushing and leaching

Now your plants are ready for the final phase: flushing and leaching. The goal of this process is to remove from the plants all the nutrients that they have received in the last three months. This is entirely necessary; if the plants are not leached properly, the final dry product will not burn correctly, and will crackle and spark when lit with a lighter. To get clean, healthy marijuana with a full aroma and taste, you must leach your plants.

On the first day of the leaching process, we do what is called a 'flush'. To flush the crop, take a hose directly to the plants and feed them water from the tap for 20 seconds. This should be done twice: as soon as your lights come on and again within a hour before they turn off. When you flush when the lights come on, they will soak all day like a dirty plate in the sink. Imagine these two actions as leaving your dirty

*The amber pistols are a sign that the plant is close to harvest.*

plates to soak in the sink, then rinsing them off afterwards. When this is completed, spray each plant with the hose for 15 seconds every other day for about a week. Once that is over, you are ready to begin harvest!

Here are pictures of the leaching phase and a finished plant. I have also included shots of my short bush style Red Devil as well, so you can see a different style of structure.

# Chapter 5

# Choosing Your Nutrients and How to Feed

## ■ Choosing your nutrients

There are many, many nutrients on the market, and with such a huge choice, it can be difficult to know which is best for your needs. There are many factors to consider before choosing any nutrient; I like to begin by looking at the manufacturer. Ideally, you should choose companies that make nutrients specifically for growing marijuana. Don't go to your local big box store and choose a big name outdoor gardening nutrient. These nutrients are cheaper but they are extremely synthetic and tend to contain lots of heavy metals, which we don't want to inhale into our bodies. You can find marijuana-friendly nutrients at an indoor growing store or on the internet. If there is no indoor growing store where you live, you can order products from the internet; but if you do have an indoor growing shop, it is best to deal with them. Remember never to order growing products to the same address as your grow.

Go to your local gardening store and see what lines of nutrients they carry. If you already have a nutrient company in mind and they do not have it, they most likely will be able to order it for you. If you don't have a specific company in mind, go online and do some research first. Start by looking at the company's web site; you are looking for companies with expensive websites and lots of info on their products. More often than not, these companies will have higher quality products. Cross-reference the information given by reading reviews of peoples' experiences with using these nutrients; growing forums are a good place to start. If you know other growers, get whatever feedback you can from them. You can also ask the store owner which product sells best. If the product is moving then it must be performing well for other people.

The next step is to decide what type of nutrients you want to grow with: organic, bio-organic, or synthetic. The nutrient company should have a line for each category.

Organic nutrients are the healthiest choice, but they are also the most expensive and tend to perform poorly when it comes to overall yield. Bio-organic nutrients are also healthy, and have decent production potential. Synthetic nutrients, which are mainly used in hydro gardens, are very unhealthy for you but result in a heavy production.

I personally utilize all three categories. I use an organic veg nutrient then a bio-organic flower nutrient with a synthetic ripening formula. In the next chapter I'll show you four growing formulas; any grow store should be able to provide you with all the products for at least one of them. Use that formula until you have mastered it, then start to change the formula to your specific liking. Any one of the four formulas in this book will give you top-notch results and all have been thoroughly tested.

How much should you spend on nutrients? I'm sure you've heard the old saying, "You get what you pay for." In marijuana growing, this is definitely true. If you choose a cheap nutrient, not even my growing techniques will get you to the higher levels of production. Your marijuana will be okay but will be slightly lower quality. Invest a little more to get a fantastic result.

## ■ Veg nutrients

As we have already learned, the first stage of growing is the vegetative cycle; you will only require one product for this period. I like the organic veg nutrients, as they give me a bushier plant to work with—but they do make the process take a little longer than if you use a bio-organic or synthetic product. I find that with bio-organic or synthetic products, it takes less time to veg, but there are not as many branches and they tend to stretch. To combat this you could use a metal halide bulb (MH), which gives off a blue light instead of the orange light given by a high-pressure sodium (HPS) bulb. The blue light will promote more branches and help prevent branch underdevelopment. One drawback of using these bulbs is that your veg cycle will be extended by an extra 30% to 40% . Also, the MH bulbs give off more heat than HPS bulbs, so extra cooling is necessary.

From cloning to your first week of your veg cycle, you should only use a 1/3 of the maximum dosage suggested on the bottle of nutrients. The plants are very delicate and small at this stage and can't handle a full dose. Once the plants are about six to eight inches tall, you can move up to 2/3 of the suggested dosage. When your plants reach one foot tall, they are big and strong enough to take a full dose.

Some growers choose to use their veg nutrient up to a couple weeks into flowering, to help the plants growth while they are turning to flower. I find that unnecessary, and like to help the flowering process as soon as possible. The natural growing pattern will give you the right size of plant for this type of indoor gardening. If you continue to use the veg nutrients, your plants may grow too big for your growing area.

## ■ Flower nutrients

The nutrient you choose for flowering is going to be your plant's main course every time they feed. I find that the organic products leave you with a less dense bud than the others. They are great if you are looking for more flavor and fairly potent buds, but most likely organics will have an effect on your final weight.

The synthetic products give you lots of flower power, both in weight and potency. However, even with an intensive leaching, you're left with street-level biker pot, which is effective but very unhealthy, especially for daily use, and will most likely leave you with a massive headache. With the bio-organic nutrients I find you get the best of worlds: great taste and great yield, plus they're much healthier than the synthetics.

Your plants will be ready for the suggested dosage on the bottle immediately, and you should use that dose for the entire flower cycle, right up until the leaching process. Always add the flower nutrient to the mixture first as a base, and then add any additional products.

## ■ Ripening nutrients

Ripening nutrients are used in the later stages of flowering, once there are flowers to ripen! It is very important that you use these products; it gives you that extra resin potency and a more dense bud. In this case, since you use only a little bit at a time with a full dose of flower nutrient, plus the proper cleaning with my leaching process, I suggest using the synthetic products. They give you that extra edge in potency and density to top off your garden before harvest. The organic and bio-organic nutrients do a great job too, but they can't compete with the synthetics' overall power. Remember to ease the ripening formula in to the feeding by starting with a small dose to start. Most ripening formulas are applied during week five to seven, or until the bud is totally ripe.

Also look for a pre-ripening product, to be used mainly during weeks three and four. Be sure to use products all from the same company, as you risk a bad reaction between the products if you don't. Do not mix companies unless you know that the products work well together. Pre-ripening formulas promote extra flowering on the branches and are also used early in the flowering process.

## ■ Leaching agents

Leaching agents were designed for hydroponic gardens, in which a lot of synthetic nutrients are used. They are necessary to remove all the excess nutrients and heavy metals that the plants have been soaking in. This is called leaching; if your plants are not leached then the resulting bud won't burn properly. I'm sure you have received bud that either crackled or left you with a black hard ash in your bowl. This means the plants were not leached and you're inhaling whatever they used on their

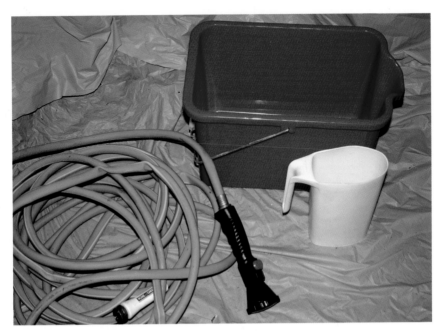

*Fifteen-liter bucket, rubber garden hose, ON/OFF switch spray attachment and a 1-quart milk container is all you will need.*

plants. Although we are growing in soil, so only really need a steady dose of plain water to leach the plants, I still like to use a leaching product as well. The cleaner your plants are, the cleaner the stone, leaving your body cleaner and increasing the flavor. Also, since many people use marijuana for medicine on a daily basis, the healthier it is, the better.

## ■ How to feed

There are many different feeding techniques, but most growers use a big reservoir; either a big plastic barrel or a large Rubbermaid container. This method is popular because it's believed to be easier and less time consuming, as they only have to make one big feeding mixture. They will then use a wand and a hose to feed the plants after they have made up their reservoir. Most will just measure the feed in a rough count as they spray the plants.

I find this method sloppy, and dangerous, and I dislike the waste of valuable nutrients and water that spill onto the floor. I do not recommend this feeding method; a reservoir holds standing water that promotes mold and pests, and the water will evaporate during the time it takes to feed again, creating extra humidity and wasting nutrients. You will also need to clean your reservoir container regularly, which is a lot of extra work.

My method will seem ridiculous to some growers, but it is less time consuming overall, more cost effective, and lets you be more intimate with the plants which will make you a better grower in the end.

You will need:

- 1 x 15-liter bucket
- 1 x milk container (which is one quart)
- 1 x rubber garden hose with a spraying attachment with an on/off switch

Simply attach the garden hose to your nearest tap and turn on the water; use room temperature water at all times. Fill up the bucket and add the nutrients. Check the pH level after you have made the mixture and ensure that it is between 5.5 and 7.5. Take the bucket and the milk container and hand feed each plant individually with the milk container. This gets your face right in to the plants so you can really see what is going on – this will happen for every feed throughout the whole process. You should be checking for under/over feeding, molds, and pests, plus it will give you a better view of your plant which will help you learn and keep on track. For a six-light garden make six to eight buckets of feed. This seems stupid to some, but trust me it will take less time, is safer, and produces no waste. For the biggest garden discussed here, which is a six-light garden, it will take about half an hour to feed; compare this to the 15 minutes it takes to make a reservoir alone. The buckets are much easier to make and allow less chance for making mistakes. If you do make a mistake it will only affect a few plants, whereas if you make a mistake with a reservoir it will affect your whole garden. Also, with my method you will only use the exact resources necessary and there is no waste. The four formulas in the next chapter are based on this feeding technique.

# Chapter 6

# Four Simple Step-by-Step Growing Formulas

All four of these formulas have been tested and all four will give you a high-grade result. I suggest you master one of the formulas first, before making any changes or trying something new. The formulas are based on the feeding system I explained in Chapter 5. The listed feeding days will be exact if room temperature and humidity is between these parameters: Lights ON: 72 to 83° F, 65% or lower. Lights OFF: 65 to 75° F, 65% or lower

## ■ Advanced Nutrients

SHAKE ALL NUTRIENTS WELL BEFORE EACH FEEDING:

V = Iguana Juice Grow          pH Level = 5.5–7.5

Plant Pot Size = 7-Gallon      Light Size and Type = 1,000-watt HPS

### ■ VEG

| Day | 1 light | 2 light | 4 light | 6 light |
|---|---|---|---|---|
| 1 | 20ml of V per 15L, 1 quart per plant | 20ml of V per 15L, 1 quart per plant | 20ml of V per 15L, 1 quart per plant | 20ml of V per 15L, 1 quart per plant |
| 4 | 20ml of V per 15L, 1 quart per plant | 20ml of V per 15L, 1 quart per plant | 20ml of V per 15L, 1 quart per plant | 20ml of V per 15L, 1 quart per plant |
| 7 | 40ml of V per 15L, 2 quarts per plant | 40ml of V per 15L, 2 quarts per plant | 40ml of V per 15L, 2 quarts per plant | 40ml of V per 15L, 2 quarts per plant |
| 10 | 40ml of V per 15L, 2 quarts per plant | 40ml of V per 15L, 2 quarts per plant | 40ml of V per 15L, 2 quarts per plant | 40ml of V per 15L, 2 quarts per plant |
| 13 | 60ml of V per 15L, 2 quarts per plant | 60ml of V per 15L, 2 quarts per plant | 60ml of V per 15L, 2 quarts per plant | 60ml of V per 15L, 2 quarts per plant |
| 16 | 60ml of V per 15L, 2 quarts per plant | 60ml of V per 15L, 2 quarts per plant | 60ml of V per 15L, 2 quarts per plant | 60ml of V per 15L, 2 quarts per plant |

Follow same instructions as day 16 until plants average 24 inches tall, 18 to 20 inches for shorter bush-style strains.

SHAKE ALL NUTRIENTS WELL BEFORE EACH FEEDING:

F = Iguana Juice Bloom          R = Overdrive

pH Level = 5.5–7.5          Plant Pot Size = 7-Gallon

Light Size and Type = 1,000 watt HPS

## ■ FLOWER week 1 and 2

| Day | 1 light | 2 light | 4 light | 6 light |
|---|---|---|---|---|
| 1 | 60–65ml of F per 15L, 3 quarts per plant | 60–65ml of F per 15L, 3 quarts per plant | 60–65ml of F per 15L, 3 quarts per plant | 60–65ml of F per 15L, 3 quarts per plant |
| 4 | 60–65ml of F per 15L, 3 quarts per plant | 60–65ml of F per 15L, 3 quarts per plant | 60–65ml of F per 15L, 3 quarts per plant | 60–65ml of F per 15L, 3 quarts per plant |
| 7 | 60–65ml of F per 15L, 3 quarts per plant | 60–65ml of F per 15L, 3 quarts per plant | 60–65ml of F per 15L, 3 quarts per plant | 60–65ml of F per 15L, 3 quarts per plant |
| 10 | 60–65ml of F per 15L, 3 quarts per plant | 60–65ml of F per 15L 3 quarts per plant | 60–65ml of F per 15L, 3 quarts per plant | 60–65ml of F per 15L, 3 quarts per plant |
| 13 | 60–65ml of F per 15L, 3 quarts per plant | 60–65ml of F per 15L, 3 quarts per plant | 60–65ml of F per 15L, 3 quarts per plant | 60–65ml of F per 15L, 3 quarts per plant |

## ■ FLOWER week 3 and 4

| Day | 1 light | 2 light | 4 light | 6 light |
|---|---|---|---|---|
| 16 | 60–65ml of F per 15L, 3 quarts per plant | 60–65ml of F per 15L, 3 quarts per plant | 60–65ml of F per 15L, 3 quarts per plant | 60–65ml of F per 15L, 3 quarts per plant |
| 18 | | | | 60–65ml of F per 15L, 3 quarts per plant |
| 19 | 60–65ml of F per 15L, 3 quarts per plant | 60–65ml of F per 15L, 3 quarts per plant | 60–65ml of F per 15L, 3 quarts per plant | |
| 20 | | | | 60–65ml of F per 15L, 3 quarts per plant |
| 22 | 60–65ml of F per 15L, 3 quarts per plant | 60–65ml of F per 15L, 3 quarts per plant | 60–65ml of F per 15L, 3 quarts per plant | 60–65ml of F per 15L, 3 quarts per plant |
| 24 | | | | 60–65ml of F per 15L, 3 quarts per plant |
| 25 | 60–65ml of F per 15L, 3 quarts per plant | 60–65ml of F per 15L, 3 quarts per plant | 60–65ml of F per 15L, 3 quarts per plant | |
| 26 | | | | 60–65ml of F per 15L, 3 quarts per plant |
| 28 | 60–65ml of F per 15L, 3 quarts per plant | 60–65ml of F per 15L, 3 quarts per plant | 60–65ml of F per 15L, 3 quarts per plant | 60–65ml of F per 15L, 3 quarts per plant |

## ■ FLOWER week 5 and 6

| Day | 1 light | 2 light | 4 light | 6 light |
|-----|---------|---------|---------|---------|
| 30 | | | | 60–65ml of F per 15L, 3 quarts per plant |
| 31 | 60–65ml of F +30ml of R per 15L, 3 quarts per plant | 60–65ml of F +30ml of R per 15L, 3 quarts per plant | 60–65ml of F +30ml of R per 15L, 3 quarts per plant | |
| 32 | | | | 60–65ml of F +30ml of R per 15L, 3 quarts per plant |
| 34 | 60–65ml of F +30ml of R per 15L, 3 quarts per plant | 60–65ml of F +30ml of R per 15L, 3 quarts per plant | 60–65ml of F +30ml of R per 15L, 3 quarts per plant | 60–65ml of F +30ml of R per 15L, 3 quarts per plant |
| 36 | | | | 60–65ml of F +30ml of R per 15L, 3 quarts per plant |
| 37 | 60–65ml of F +30ml of R per 15L, 3 quarts per plant | 60–65ml of F +30ml of R per 15L, 3 quarts per plant | 60–65ml of F +30ml of R per 15L, 3 quarts per plant | |
| 38 | | | | 60–65ml of F +30ml of R per 15L, 3 quarts per plant |
| 40 | 60–65ml of F +30ml of R per 15L, 3 quarts per plant | 60–65ml of F +30ml of R per 15L, 3 quarts per plant | 60–65ml of F +30ml of R per 15L, 3 quarts per plant | 60–65ml of F +30ml of R per 15L, 3 quarts per plant |

FLUSH DAY = Spray each plant with hose for 20 seconds as soon as lights come on and again within one hour before lights turn off. (Mop up after each session.)

## ■ FLOWER week 7 and 8

| Day | 1 light | 2 light | 4 light | 6 light |
|---|---|---|---|---|
| 42 | | | | 60–65ml of F +30ml of R per 15L, 3 quarts per plant |
| 43 | 60–65ml of F +30ml of R per 15L, 3 quarts per plant | 60–65ml of F +30ml of R per 15L, 3 quarts per plant | 60–65ml of F +30ml of R per 15L, 3 quarts per plant | |
| 44 | | | | 60–65ml of F +30ml of R per 15L, 3 quarts per plant |
| 46 | 60–65ml of F +30ml of R per 15L, 3 quarts per plant | 60–65ml of F +30ml of R per 15L, 3 quarts per plant | 60–65ml of F +30ml of R per 15L, 3 quarts per plant | 60–65ml of F +30ml of R per 15L, 3 quarts per plant |

If your strain requires more time, continue with last step until flowers have finished ripening then continue.

| Day | 1 light | 2 light | 4 light | 6 light |
|---|---|---|---|---|
| 48 | Flush Day | Flush Day | Flush Day | Flush Day |
| 50 | 3 quarts of plain water per plant | 3 quarts of plain water per plant | 3 quarts of plain water per plant | 3 quarts of plain water per plant |
| 52 | 3 quarts of plain water per plant | 3 quarts of plain water per plant | 3 quarts of plain water per plant | 3 quarts of plain water per plant |
| 54 | 3 quarts of plain water per plant | 3 quarts of plain water per plant | 3 quarts of plain water per plant | 3 quarts of plain water per plant |
| 56 | Harvest | Harvest | Harvest | Harvest |

## ■ Botanicare

SHAKE ALL NUTRIENTS WELL BEFORE EACH FEEDING:

V = Pure Blend Pro Grow    pH Level = 5.5–7.5

Plant Pot Size = 7-Gallon    Light Size and Type = 1,000-watt HPS

### ■ VEG

| Day | 1 light | 2 light | 4 light | 6 light |
|---|---|---|---|---|
| 1 | 30ml of V per 15L, 1 quart per plant | 30ml of V per 15L, 1 quart per plant | 30ml of V per 15L, 1 quart per plant | 30ml of V per 15L, 1 quart per plant |
| 4 | 30ml of V per 15L, 1 quart per plant | 30ml of V per 15L, 1 quart per plant | 30ml of V per 15L, 1 quart per plant | 30ml of V per 15L, 1 quart per plant |
| 7 | 40ml of V per 15L, 2 quarts per plant | 40ml of V per 15L, 2 quarts per plant | 40ml of V per 15L, 2 quarts per plant | 40ml of V per 15L, 2 quarts per plant |
| 10 | 40ml of V per 15L, 2 quarts per plant | 40ml of V per 15L, 2 quarts per plant | 40ml of V per 15L, 2 quarts per plant | 40ml of V per 15L, 2 quarts per plant |
| 13 | 60ml of V per 15L, 2 quarts per plant | 60ml of V per 15L, 2 quarts per plant | 60ml of V per 15L, 2 quarts per plant | 60ml of V per 15L, 2 quarts per plant |
| 16 | 100ml of V per 15L, 2 quarts per plant | 100ml of V per 15L, 2 quarts per plant | 100ml of V per 15L, 2 quarts per plant | 100ml of V per 15L, 2 quarts per plant |

Follow same instructions as day 16 until plants are average 24 inches tall, 18 to 20 inches for shorter bush style strains

SHAKE ALL NUTRIENTS WELL BEFORE EACH FEEDING:

F = Pure Blend Pro Bloom (soil)    R = CNS17 Ripe

pH Level = 5.5–7.5    Plant Pot Size = 7-Gallon

Light Size and Type = 1,000-watt HPS

### ■ FLOWER week 1 and 2

| Day | 1 light | 2 light | 4 light | 6 light |
|---|---|---|---|---|
| 1 | 100ml of F per 15L, 3 quarts per plant | 100ml of F per 15L, 3 quarts per plant | 100ml of F per 15L, 3 quarts per plant | 100ml of F per 15L, 3 quarts per plant |
| 4 | 100ml of F per 15L, 3 quarts per plant | 100ml of F per 15L, 3 quarts per plant | 100ml of F per 15L, 3 quarts per plant | 100ml of F per 15L, 3 quarts per plant |
| 7 | 100ml of F per 15L, 3 quarts per plant | 100ml of F per 15L, 3 quarts per plant | 100ml of F per 15L, 3 quarts per plant | 100ml of F per 15L, 3 quarts per plant |
| 10 | 100ml of F per 15L, 3 quarts per plant | 100ml of F per 15L, 3 quarts per plant | 100ml of F per 15L, 3 quarts per plant | 100ml of F per 15L, 3 quarts per plant |
| 13 | 100ml of F per 15L, 3 quarts per plant | 100ml of F per 15L, 3 quarts per plant | 100ml of F per 15L, 3 quarts per plant | 100ml of F per 15L, 3 quarts per plant |

## ■ FLOWER week 3 and 4

| Day | 1 light | 2 light | 4 light | 6 light |
|-----|---------|---------|---------|---------|
| 16 | 100ml of F per 15L, 3 quarts per plant | 100ml of F per 15L, 3 quarts per plant | 100ml of F per 15L, 3 quarts per plant | 100ml of F per 15L, 3 quarts per plant |
| 18 | | | | 100ml of F per 15L, 3 quarts per plant |
| 19 | 100ml of F per 15L, 3 quarts per plant | 100ml of F per 15L, 3 quarts per plant | 100ml of F per 15L, 3 quarts per plant | |
| 20 | | | | 100ml of F per 15L, 3 quarts per plant |
| 22 | 100ml of F per 15L, 3 quarts per plant | 100ml of F per 15L, 3 quarts per plant | 100ml of F per 15L, 3 quarts per plant | 100ml of F per 15L, 3 quarts per plant |
| 24 | | | | 100ml of F per 15L, 3 quarts per plant |
| 25 | 100ml of F per 15L, 3 quarts per plant | 100ml of F per 15L, 3 quarts per plant | 100ml of F per 15L, 3 quarts per plant | |
| 26 | | | | 100ml of F per 15L, 3 quarts per plant |
| 28 | 100ml of F per 15L, 3 quarts per plant | 100ml of F per 15L, 3 quarts per plant | 100ml of F per 15L, 3 quarts per plant | 100ml of F per 15L, 3 quarts per plant |

## ■ FLOWER week 3 and 4

| Day | 1 light | 2 light | 4 light | 6 light |
|---|---|---|---|---|
| 30 | | | | 100ml of F per 15L, 3 quarts per plant |
| 31 | 100ml of F +50ml of R per 15L, 3 quarts per plant | 100ml of F +50ml of R per 15L, 3 quarts per plant | 100ml of F +50ml of R per 15L, 3 quarts per plant | |
| 32 | | | | 100ml of F +50ml of R per 15L, 3 quarts per plant |
| 34 | 100ml of F +100ml of R per 15L, 3 quarts per plant | 100ml of F +100ml of R per 15L, 3 quarts per plant | 100ml of F +100ml of R per 15L, 3 quarts per plant | 100ml of F +100ml of R per 15L, 3 quarts per plant |
| 36 | | | | 100ml of F +100ml of R per 15L, 3 quarts per plant |
| 37 | 100ml of F +100ml of R per 15L, 3 quarts per plant | 100ml of F +100ml of R per 15L, 3 quarts per plant | 100ml of F +100ml of R per 15L, 3 quarts per plant | |
| 38 | | | | 100 ml of F +100 ml of R per 15L, 3 quarts per plant |
| 40 | 100ml of F +100ml of R per 15L, 3 quarts per plant | 100ml of F +100ml of R per 15L, 3 quarts per plant | 100ml of F +100ml of R per 15L, 3 quarts per plant | 100ml of F +100ml of R per 15L, 3 quarts per plant3 |

FLUSH DAY = Spray each plant with hose for 20 seconds, as soon as lights come on and again within one hour before lights turn off. (Mop up after each session.)

## ■ FLOWER week 7 and 8

| Day | 1 light | 2 light | 4 light | 6 light |
|---|---|---|---|---|
| 42 | | | | 100ml of F<br>+100ml of R per 15L,<br>3 quarts per plant |
| 43 | 100ml of F<br>+100ml of R per 15L,<br>3 quarts per plant | 100ml of F<br>+100ml of R per 15L,<br>3 quarts per plant | 100ml of F<br>+100ml of R per 15L,<br>3 quarts per plant | |
| 44 | | | | 100ml of F<br>+100ml of R per 15L,<br>3 quarts per plant |
| 46 | 100ml of F<br>+100ml of R per 15L,<br>3 quarts per plant | 100ml of F<br>+100ml of R per 15L,<br>3 quarts per plant | 100ml of F<br>+100ml of R per 15L,<br>3 quarts per plant | 100ml of F<br>+100ml of R per 15L,<br>3 quarts per plant |

If your strain requires more time, continue with last step until flowers have finished ripening, then continue.

| Day | 1 light | 2 light | 4 light | 6 light |
|---|---|---|---|---|
| 48 | Flush Day | Flush Day | Flush Day | Flush Day |
| 50 | 3 quarts of plain water per plant | 3 quarts of plain water per plant | 3 quarts of plain water per plant | 3 quarts of plain water per plant |
| 52 | 3 quarts of plain water per plant | 3 quarts of plain water per plant | 3 quarts of plain water per plant | 3 quarts of plain water per plant |
| 54 | 3 quarts of plain water per plant | 3 quarts of plain water per plant | 3 quarts of plain water per plant | 3 quarts of plain water per plant |
| 56 | Harvest | Harvest | Harvest | Harvest |

# ■ Canna

SHAKE ALL NUTRIENTS WELL BEFORE EACH FEEDING:

V = Terra Vega                          pH Level = 5.5–7.5

Plant Pot Size = 7-Gallon          Light Size and Type = 1,000-watt HPS

## ■ VEG

| Day | 1 light | 2 light | 4 light | 6 light |
|---|---|---|---|---|
| 1 | 25ml of V per 15L, 1 quart per plant | 25ml of V per 15L, 1 quart per plant | 25ml of V per 15L, 1 quart per plant | 25ml of V per 15L, 1 quart per plant |
| 4 | 25ml of V per 15L, 1 quart per plant | 25ml of V per 15L, 1 quart per plant | 25ml of V per 15L, 1 quart per plant | 25ml of V per 15L, 1 quart per plant |
| 7 | 50ml of V per 15L, 2 quarts per plant | 50ml of V per 15L, 2 quarts per plant | 50ml of V per 15L, 2 quarts per plant | 50ml of V per 15L, 2 quarts per plant |
| 10 | 50ml of V per 15L, 2 quarts per plant | 50ml of V per 15L, 2 quarts per plant | 50ml of V per 15L, 2 quarts per plant | 50ml of V per 15L, 2 quarts per plant |
| 13 | 75ml of V per 15L, 2 quarts per plant | 75ml of V per 15L, 2 quarts per plant | 75ml of V per 15L, 2 quarts per plant | 75ml of V per 15L, 2 quarts per plant |
| 16 | 75ml of V per 15L, 2 quarts per plant | 75ml of V per 15L, 2 quarts per plant | 75ml of V per 15L, 2 quarts per plant | 75ml of V per 15L, 2 quarts per plant |

Follow same instructions as day 16 until plants are average 24 inches tall or 18 to 20 inches for shorter bush-style strains.

SHAKE ALL NUTRIENTS WELL BEFORE EACH FEEDING:

F = Terra Flores                        R = Canna Boost

pH Level = 5.5–7.5                    Plant Pot Size = 7-Gallon

Light Size and Type = 1,000-watt HPS

## ■ FLOWER week 1 and 2

| Day | 1 light | 2 light | 4 light | 6 light |
|---|---|---|---|---|
| 1 | 75ml of F per 15L, 3 quarts per plant | 75ml of F per 15L, 3 quarts per plant | 75ml of F per 15L, 3 quarts per plant | 75ml of F per 15L, 3 quarts per plant |
| 4 | 75ml of F per 15L, 3 quarts per plant | 75ml of F per 15L, 3 quarts per plant | 75ml of F per 15L, 3 quarts per plant | 75ml of F per 15L, 3 quarts per plant |
| 7 | 75ml of F per 15L, 3 quarts per plant | 75ml of F per 15L, 3 quarts per plant | 75ml of F per 15L, 3 quarts per plant | 75ml of F per 15L, 3 quarts per plant |
| 10 | 75ml of F per 15L, 3 quarts per plant | 75ml of F per 15L, 3 quarts per plant | 75ml of F per 15L, 3 quarts per plant | 75ml of F per 15L, 3 quarts per plant |
| 13 | 75ml of F per 15L, 3 quarts per plant | 75ml of F per 15L, 3 quarts per plant | 75ml of F per 15L, 3 quarts per plant | 75ml of F per 15L, 3 quarts per plant |

## ■ FLOWER week 3 and 4

| Day | 1 light | 2 light | 4 light | 6 light |
|---|---|---|---|---|
| 16 | 75ml of F per 15L, 3 quarts per plant | 75ml of F per 15L, 3 quarts per plant | 75ml of F per 15L, 3 quarts per plant | 75ml of F per 15L, 3 quarts per plant |
| 18 | | | | 75ml of F per 15L, 3 quarts per plant |
| 19 | 75ml of F per 15L, 3 quarts per plant | 75ml of F per 15L, 3 quarts per plant | 75ml of F per 15L, 3 quarts per plant | |
| 20 | | | | 75ml of F per 15L, 3 quarts per plant |
| 22 | 75ml of F per 15L, 3 quarts per plant | 75ml of F per 15L, 3 quarts per plant | 75ml of F per 15L, 3 quarts per plant | 75ml of F per 15L, 3 quarts per plant |
| 24 | | | | 75ml of F per 15L, 3 quarts per plant |
| 25 | 75ml of F per 15L, 3 quarts per plant | 75ml of F per 15L, 3 quarts per plant | 75ml of F per 15L, 3 quarts per plant | |
| 26 | | | | 75ml of F per 15L, 3 quarts per plant |
| 28 | 75ml of F per 15L, 3 quarts per plant | 75ml of F per 15L, 3 quarts per plant | 75ml of F per 15L, 3 quarts per plant | 75ml of F per 15L, 3 quarts per plant |

## ■ FLOWER week 5 and 6

| Day | 1 light | 2 light | 4 light | 6 light |
|---|---|---|---|---|
| 30 | | | | 75ml of F per 15L, 3 quarts per plant |
| 31 | 75ml of F +25ml of R per 15L, 3 quarts per plant | 75ml of F +25ml of R per 15L, 3 quarts per plant | 75ml of F +25ml of R per 15L, 3 quarts per plant | |
| 32 | | | | 75ml of F +25ml of R per 15L, 3 quarts per plant |
| 34 | 75ml of F +25ml of R per 15L, 3 quarts per plant | 75ml of F +25ml of R per 15L, 3 quarts per plant | 75ml of F +25ml of R per 15L, 3 quarts per plant | 75ml of F +25ml of R per 15L, 3 quarts per plant |
| 36 | | | | 75ml of F +25ml of R per 15L, 3 quarts per plant |
| 37 | 75ml of F +50ml of R per 15L, 3 quarts per plant | 75ml of F +50ml of R per 15L, 3 quarts per plant | 75ml of F +50ml of R per 15L, 3 quarts per plant | |
| 38 | | | | 75ml of F +50ml of R per 15L, 3 quarts per plant |
| 40 | 75ml of F +50ml of R per 15L, 3 quarts per plant | 75ml of F +50ml of R per 15L, 3 quarts per plant | 75ml of F +50ml of R per 15L, 3 quarts per plant | 75ml of F +50ml of R per 15L, 3 quarts per plant |

FLUSH DAY = Spray each plant with hose for 20 seconds as soon as lights come on and again within one hour before lights turn off. (Mop up after each session.)

## ■ FLOWER week 7 and 8

| Day | 1 light | 2 light | 4 light | 6 light |
|---|---|---|---|---|
| 42 | | | | 75ml of F +50ml of R per 15L, 3 quarts per plant |
| 43 | 75ml of F +50ml of R per 15L, 3 quarts per plant | 75ml of F +50ml of R per 15L, 3 quarts per plant | 75ml of F +50ml of R per 15L, 3 quarts per plant | |
| 44 | | | | 75ml of F +50ml of R per 15L, 3 quarts per plant |
| 46 | 75ml of F +50ml of R per 15L, 3 quarts per plant | 75ml of F +50ml of R per 15L, 3 quarts per plant | 75ml of F +50ml of R per 15L, 3 quarts per plant | 75ml of F +50ml of R per 15L, 3 quarts per plant |

If your strain requires more time, continue with last step until flowers have finished ripening, then continue.

| Day | 1 light | 2 light | 4 light | 6 light |
|---|---|---|---|---|
| 48 | Flush Day | Flush Day | Flush Day | Flush Day |
| 50 | 3 quarts of plain water per plant | 3 quarts of plain water per plant | 3 quarts of plain water per plant | 3 quarts of plain water per plant |
| 52 | 3 quarts of plain water per plant | 3 quarts of plain water per plant | 3 quarts of plain water per plant | 3 quarts of plain water per plant |
| 54 | 3 quarts of plain water per plant | 3 quarts of plain water per plant | 3 quarts of plain water per plant | 3 quarts of plain water per plant |
| 56 | Harvest | Harvest | Harvest | Harvest |

# ■ General Hydroponics

SHAKE ALL NUTRIENTS WELL BEFORE EACH FEEDING:

V = FloraNova Grow  pH Level = 5.5–7.5

Plant Pot Size = 7-Gallon  Light Size and Type = 1,000-watt HPS

## ■ VEG

| Day | 1 light | 2 light | 4 light | 6 light |
|---|---|---|---|---|
| 1 | 20ml of V per 15L, 1 quart per plant | 20ml of V per 15L, 1 quart per plant | 20ml of V per 15L, 1 quart per plant | 20ml of V per 15L, 1 quart per plant |
| 4 | 20ml ml of V per 15L, 1 quart per plant | 20ml ml of V per 15L, 1 quart per plant | 20ml ml of V per 15L, 1 quart per plant | 20ml ml of V per 15L, 1 quart per plant |
| 7 | 40ml of V per 15L, 2 quarts per plant | 40ml of V per 15L, 2 quarts per plant | 40ml of V per 15L, 2 quarts per plant | 40ml of V per 15L, 2 quarts per plant |
| 10 | 40ml of V per 15L, 2 quarts per plant | 40ml of V per 15L, 2 quarts per plant | 40ml of V per 15L, 2 quarts per plant | 40ml of V per 15L, 2 quarts per plant |
| 13 | 60ml of V per 15L, 2 quarts per plant | 60ml of V per 15L, 2 quarts per plant | 60ml of V per 15L, 2 quarts per plant | 60ml of V per 15L, 2 quarts per plant |
| 16 | 60ml of V per 15L, 2 quarts per plant | 60ml of V per 15L, 2 quarts per plant | 60ml of V per 15L, 2 quarts per plant | 60ml of V per 15L, 2 quarts per plant |

Follow same instructions as day 16 until plants average 24 inches tall, 18 to 20 inches for shorter bush-style strains.

SHAKE ALL NUTRIENTS WELL BEFORE EACH FEEDING:

F = FloraNova Bloom  R = Kool Bloom (Dry)

pH Level = 5.5–7.5  Plant Pot Size = 7-Gallon

Light Size and Type = 1,000-watt HPS

## ■ FLOWER week 1 and 2

| Day | 1 light | 2 light | 4 light | 6 light |
|---|---|---|---|---|
| 1 | 60ml of F per 15L, 3 quarts per plant | 60ml of F per 15L, 3 quarts per plant | 60ml of F per 15L, 3 quarts per plant | 60ml of F per 15L, 3 quarts per plant |
| 4 | 60ml of F per 15L, 3 quarts per plant | 60ml of F per 15L, 3 quarts per plant | 60ml of F per 15L, 3 quarts per plant | 60ml of F per 15L, 3 quarts per plant |
| 7 | 60ml of F per 15L, 3 quarts per plant | 60ml of F per 15L, 3 quarts per plant | 60ml of F per 15L, 3 quarts per plant | 60ml of F per 15L, 3 quarts per plant |
| 10 | 60ml of F per 15L, 3 quarts per plant | 60ml of F per 15L, 3 quarts per plant | 60ml of F per 15L, 3 quarts per plant | 60ml of F per 15L, 3 quarts per plant |
| 13 | 60ml of F per 15L, 3 quarts per plant | 60ml of F per 15L, 3 quarts per plant | 60ml of F per 15L, 3 quarts per plant | 60ml of F per 15L, 3 quarts per plant |

## ■ FLOWER week 3 and 4

| Day | 1 light | 2 light | 4 light | 6 light |
|-----|---------|---------|---------|---------|
| 16 | 60ml of F per 15L, 3 quarts per plant | 60ml of F per 15L, 3 quarts per plant | 60ml of F per 15L, 3 quarts per plant | 60ml of F per 15L, 3 quarts per plant |
| 18 | | | | 60ml of F per 15L, 3 quarts per plant |
| 19 | 60ml of F per 15L, 3 quarts per plant | 60ml of F per 15L, 3 quarts per plant | 60ml of F per 15L, 3 quarts per plant | |
| 20 | | | | 60ml of F per 15L, 3 quarts per plant |
| 22 | 60ml of F per 15L, 3 quarts per plant | 60ml of F per 15L, 3 quarts per plant | 60ml of F per 15L, 3 quarts per plant | 60ml of F per 15L, 3 quarts per plant |
| 24 | | | | 60ml of F per 15L, 3 quarts per plant |
| 25 | 60ml of F per 15L, 3 quarts per plant | 60ml of F per 15L, 3 quarts per plant | 60ml of F per 15L, 3 quarts per plant | |
| 26 | | | | 60ml of F per 15L, 3 quarts per plant |
| 28 | 60ml of F per 15L, 3 quarts per plant | 60ml of F per 15L, 3 quarts per plant | 60ml of F per 15L, 3 quarts per plant | 60ml of F per 15L, 3 quarts per plant |

## ■ FLOWER week 5 and 6

| Day | 1 light | 2 light | 4 light | 6 light |
|---|---|---|---|---|
| 30 | | | | 60ml of F per 15L, 3 quarts per plant |
| 31 | 60ml of F +1 Tbsp of R per 15L, 3 quarts per plant | 60ml of F +1 Tbsp of R per 15L, 3 quarts per plant | 60ml of F +1 Tbsp of R per 15L, 3 quarts per plant | |
| 32 | | | | 60ml of F +1 Tbsp of R per 15L, 3 quarts per plant |
| 34 | 60ml of F +25ml of R per 15L, 3 quarts per plant | 60ml of F +25ml of R per 15L, 3 quarts per plant | 60ml of F +25ml of R per 15L, 3 quarts per plant | 60ml of F +25ml of R per 15L, 3 quarts per plant |
| 36 | | | | 60ml of F +1 Tbsp of R per 15L, 3 quarts per plant |
| 37 | 60ml of F +1 Tbsp of R per 15L, 3 quarts per plant | 60ml of F +1 Tbsp of R per 15L, 3 quarts per plant | 60ml of F +1 Tbsp of R per 15L, 3 quarts per plant | |
| 38 | | | | 60ml of F +2 Tbsps of R per 15L, 3 quarts per plant |
| 40 | 60ml of F +2 Tbsps of R per 15L, 3 quarts per plant | 60ml of F +2 Tbsps of R per 15L, 3 quarts per plant | 60ml of F +2 Tbsps of R per 15L, 3 quarts per plant | 60ml of F +2 Tbsps of R per 15L, 3 quarts per plant |

FLUSH DAY = Spray each plant with hose for 20 seconds as soon as lights come on and again within one hour before lights turn off. (Mop up after each session.)

## ■ FLOWER week 7 and 8

| Day | 1 light | 2 light | 4 light | 6 light |
|---|---|---|---|---|
| 42 | | | | 60ml of F +2 Tbsps of R per 15L, 3 quarts per plant |
| 43 | 60ml of F +2 Tbsps of R per 15L, 3 quarts per plant | 60ml of F +2 Tbsps of R per 15L, 3 quarts per plant | 60ml of F +2 Tbsps of R per 15L, 3 quarts per plant | |
| 44 | | | | 60ml of F +2 Tbsps of R per 15L, 3 quarts per plant |
| 46 | 60ml of F +2 Tbsps of R per 15L, 3 quarts per plant | 60ml of F +2 Tbsps of R per 15L, 3 quarts per plant | 60ml of F +2 Tbsps of R per 15L, 3 quarts per plant | 60ml of F +2 Tbsps of R per 15L, 3 quarts per plant |

If your strain requires more time, continue with last step until flowers have finished ripening then continue.

| Day | 1 light | 2 light | 4 light | 6 light |
|---|---|---|---|---|
| 48 | Flush Day | Flush Day | Flush Day | Flush Day |
| 50 | 3 quarts of plain water per plant | 3 quarts of plain water per plant | 3 quarts of plain water per plant | 3 quarts of plain water per plant |
| 52 | 3 quarts of plain water per plant | 3 quarts of plain water per plant | 3 quarts of plain water per plant | 3 quarts of plain water per plant |
| 54 | 3 quarts of plain water per plant | 3 quarts of plain water per plant | 3 quarts of plain water per plant | 3 quarts of plain water per plant |
| 56 | Harvest | Harvest | Harvest | Harvest |

# Chapter 7

# Upgrade Yielding

## ■ What is upgrade yielding?

When I received my first medical marijuana production license, it covered a 15-plant grow. To set this up, I used one 1,000-watt HPS light and had my plants in small two-gallon pots. All I could get was a pound and a half of finished product per grow, forcing me to grow all year around. This was not working out, plus I needed more than the three grams a day. My doctor agreed to raise it to a 25-plant license. He did not feel comfortable in giving me any more even though it was needed, because the government could have created problems for him. I planted the 25 plants in two-gallon pots under the same 1,000-watt HPS light, expecting a significant increase. All I got was the same pound and a half.

I came to the conclusion that you can only grow so much per square footage of light, regardless of how many plants are under the light. My next step was to add a second light, then spread the same 25 plants in two-gallon pots under those two lights. The result of this grow was just shy of three pounds. Finally I was heading in the right direction, but I still had to grow all year round in order to keep myself supplied. The next step was going to four lights with the same 25 plants. This time I got rid of the two-gallon pots, and used seven-gallon pots to increase the size of the plants, since I was only going to have six plants under each light. This gave me over five pounds of finished product with each grow. With this setup I only had to grow twice a year to keep myself fully stocked.

Finally, as shown in Chapters Three and Four, using six 1,000-watt HPS lights, I spread out the same 25 plants in seven-gallon pots: four plants per light and one mother. The final result was almost nine pounds of finished product; I only have to grow this garden once a year to get a year's supply. This is "Upgrade yielding"; taking the same limited number of plants and increasing your yield by increasing your the square footage of light.

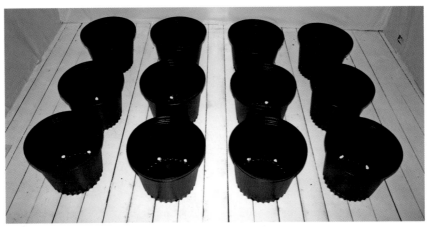

## ■ Directions

### Two-light setup

For a two-light setup, I suggest using a seven-gallon pot right away. You will only use six plants per light instead of 12, but you will get the same result. It is easier to take care of 12 plants than 25, and since your plants will grow larger in the seven-gallon pots, they will give you more prime flowers for your supply. This also makes harvest a lot easier; harvesting 25 smaller plants can be tedious and time consuming. Remember, your final yield is dependent on square footage of light, not how many plants you have. The setup is simple: place the pots in three rows of four, centered under the two lights, as shown. You should get about three pounds of finished product. When growing in pots, a pound and a half per light is a very good yield.

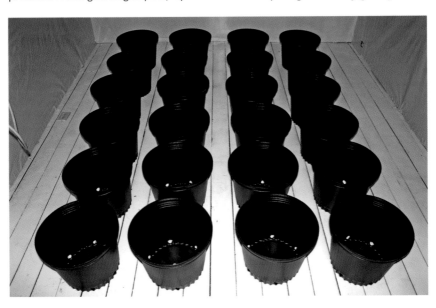

## Four-light setup

If you're using the four-light setup you will need to use 25 plants; 24 for the production garden and one mother for your cloning garden. Still using the seven-gallon pots, you just spread the 24 under the four 1,000-watt HPS lights. This will mean six plants per light. Make six rows of four plants, centered under the four lights as shown. Your final result with this should be well over five pounds of finished product.

## Six-light setup

The six-light setup is as large as I would go with a 25-plant license. You could go up to an eight-light setup with 1,000-watt HPS lights, but the numbers with expansion will start to decrease. For this setup, take the seven-gallon pots, and make the same six rows of four plants. This time just spread them out evenly under the six lights, making more space between each plant than there is in the four-light setup. Your plants will fill the whole growing area, leaving you with at least eight to nine pounds of bud or even more. This garden produces almost twice as much as a four-light setup, but it is also twice as hard to take care of. Feeding takes place every other day instead of every three days, with more buckets of nutrients to feed.

# Chapter 8

# Harvest

## ■ Drying room setup

Before you can begin harvest, you must first create space to hang-dry your harvested bud, and to do this we will change your growing room in to a drying room. Take two eight-foot 2x4s and screw in ten ceiling hooks eight to ten inches apart, then screw them onto both walls close to the ceiling. This will give you ten lines to use for hanging, each one about ten feet each in length. This will be just enough line for all of the pieces to hang. If you are only growing with four lights you will need only half that, and a two light garden will only need a quarter. Next wrap hemp rope or natural twine around the ceiling hooks to make a good strong line. I find that the hemp rope works best and holds very well; if you are going to use anything else, I suggest wire. Basically, the lines need to be just as tough as an outdoor clothing line used to dry clothes.

# ■ Trimming

Now that the hanging garden is complete, you are ready to start trimming. Trimming is when you manicure the buds using scissors or a trimming machine; I will show you how to use both with this method. This is done before the bud begins to dry (1) because it is much easier to trim and (2) when the pieces are hung, the THC (the good stuff) remaining in the stalk pours into the bud, so you don't want to waste that by trimming it off after the process is done.

## Step 1

Using a plant-cutter, cut the main stalk at its base and place on a table. Next you want to break up the plant in to several pieces so it is easier to work with.

## Step 2

To make little hooks on the pieces for hanging, cut the bottom of the plant and make your way to the top. Cut above each branch but in between the next branch, which will leave you with a hook.

## Step 3

Now prep each piece for trimming by pulling off all fan leaves by hand.

## Step 4

Take a pair of scissors and, starting from the bottom, manicure each section as close to the bud as you can.

## Step 5

Once you have filled a container with trimmed pieces, hang each piece on the line. It is okay for the pieces to be touching.

## ■ Trimming with machines

Trimming with scissors is very long and tedious. For a crop this size I strongly suggest you invest in a tabletop trimming machine. They are very easy to use and will turn a two or four day job into a two or four hour job. Follow the same first three steps as in the scissors method before you do anything else. The trimming machine has a steel grid that you place your bud on; underneath the steel grid is a fan with blades that sucks the leaf into the machine and cuts, leaving you with a manicured piece. The trimmings are then dropped in a catch bag, leaving you with minimal

clean up. As shown in the pictures, you just place your piece on top of the grill and slowly roll it until it is trimmed all around. Be very careful not to stick your fingers in the grill and always wear safety glasses when using this machine.

## ■ Room control

After every last piece is trimmed and hanged, the bud is ready to be dried. The ideal conditions for this are the same as the grow room when the lights were on. The room should never be hotter than 78° F as the bud will dry too quickly; a steady 75° F with humidity lower than 60% will dry bud perfectly in about four days. For best results while drying, keep the hanging garden in the dark at all times; this will help the process and let all of the pieces dry evenly. Also, use an oscillating fan on low to give a slight breeze over your hanging pieces. Above are some photos of the hanging garden from the crop we are following in this book.

## ■ When are my hanging pieces ready?

In order to start the next phase of harvest, you have to determine that your pieces are dry enough. After the bud has been drying for about three days in the conditions outlined above, go up to random pieces and bend the stalk. If the bend in the stalk stays in one piece, the crop is not ready. If the pieces you checked snap into two, you have let it dry to long or had too much heat in the room. If the pieces snap but still stay together, then they are ready to begin the curing phase. Try not to base your decision on how dry the bud feels, as this will change later in the curing phase.

## ■ Snipping

Snipping is when you quite simply snip each bud on your hanging pieces off into an air-sealed bucket. You can find these five-gallon buckets and lids at any grow store. I will show you how to use them later in this chapter. Once again, take each piece and work from the bottom to the top, snipping each flower off the stalk in to your buckets. When you reach the top bud on the stalk, snip it into one piece.

# ■ Curing

The bud is now ready to be cured. Curing is basically when you bring out as much THC and flavor as possible. It will also complete the drying stage and make the cannabis ready for use. Just as with wine, the longer the bud has to cure, the better it will be. Use air-sealed buckets to cure the bud, as they pull any water left inside the stem back into the bud; this is called sweating. If you decide to just bag it and not use the buckets, the bud will eventually sweat on its own and, if left in the bag, become moldy.

## Step 1

Fill three quarters of each bucket with your bud.

## Step 2

Press each lip of the lid down until you have one tiny gap left to close.

## Step 3

Place your foot on top of the bucket and press down. You should hear a little swoosh (that is the rest of the air coming out of the bucket), then quickly seal the last opening.

## Step 4

Leave the buckets sealed for at least 24 hours to give the buds chance to sweat. After 24 hours, check the moisture of your bud by taking the lid off the bucket and feeling on the inside for moisture. If there is none, then stir the bucket and reseal as shown above for another 24 hours. If, after three days, your bud is still bone-dry then it was dried for too long during the hanging phase. It is, however, ready to be used and stored.

## Step 5

If your bud started to sweat, it now needs to be dried again. To do this, leave the lids off, and stir the bucket every half an hour until it is crispy to the touch.

The dryness of your bud when it's first placed in the buckets will determine how many times it will sweat. To determine when it will stop sweating, take a piece out of the bucket and break the little stem sticking out of the bud. Just as I explained before, if the stem just bends and stays together, you're not done sweating. If the stem breaks but is still together, then just make sure the bud is dry on the outside. If so, it's ready for use and storage.

## ■ Testing

Bud has to be nice and clean before it's used. The best way to check this is to do a 'burn test' using a pipe or a bong. Light up your bowl and listen for any crackling from the bowl while you toke; there should be none. Finish smoking the entire bowl; the color of the ash left will tell you how clean the bud is. If the ash is black and hard then your bud is really dirty and will have to be emergency flushed, which I will explain below. If your ash is grey and soft, then your bud is clean enough for use – enjoy! If you followed all the steps correctly then your ash should be bright white and, if blown on or touched, it should turn to dust. You can use this method to ascertain if your each subsequent crop is getting cleaner. Simply put, the whiter the ash is, the cleaner it is. You will also be able to tell how clean your bud is by how clean the effects are. Above is a picture of some clean Blastaberry.

# ■ Emergency flush

Warning: only do this if your ash is black and hard and will barely burn.

### Step 1

Fill a container 2/3 full with distilled water. The container can be any size, depending on how much bud you are going to clean.

### Step 2

Pour in the bud and make sure it is completely emerged in the distilled water.

### Step 3

Soak all of the bud in the distilled water for a minimum of three to four hours.

## Step 4

Take a strainer and scoop out all of the bud that was soaking.

## Step 5

Lay it all out on a table and leave until it is dry and crispy to the touch.

This technique can take even greatly overfed bud that was never leached and turn it into the smoothest toke you ever had.

## ■ Storing your bud

If, when you bend the bud stalks, they snap but stay together, your bud is ready to be stored. Take out what you need for a few weeks and store it in an airtight Mason jar for you to pick out of. Leave the rest in the buckets for as long as possible, checking them once a week and giving them a good stir. For best results, keep the buckets

in a cool dark spot. The longer your bud stays in the buckets the better it will age and smoke. If you are not willing to do that for whatever reason, then seal the bud in freezer bags and leave it in the freezer.

The final net weight of the Blastaberry test crop pictured in this book was 8.5 pounds. Above is a picture of the final product.

# Chapter 9

# Pest, Disease, Mold and Odor Control

## ■ Odor prevention and techniques

If you followed the garden designs in this book, then odor should not be an issue for you. However, each garden is different, so here are some techniques I have used over the years to combat any odor issues that might come up.

If your garden is expelling a lot of suspicious smells, it could make your happy home into a serious target, so reducing the odor is imperative. Deal first with the odor outside your garden. If you can smell your pot outside, cap all exhaust fans with a charcoal filter. This should eliminate the smell outdoors entirely. Other than that, there should never be an odor outside of your residence; inside, however, is a different story. Some things I have used to combat indoor stink include the automatic sprayers you might find in a public washroom. They are made for home use now and there are many different scents to choose from; simply put in the batteries  and cartridge and hang them on the wall in an area near the entrance of your garden. This will definitely mask the odor inside your residence for 24 hours a day. A potpourri cooker in the house is also another very effective method, but don't waste your time with scented candles as they could end up doing more harm than good and constantly need to be replaced, which is expensive. I also don't recommend burning incense, as this also has to be constantly replaced and monitored, and furthermore there is a

stereotype that links people who burn incense to people who smoke marijuana. To me it's a dead giveaway.

For controlling odor inside your garden, which of course will stop it from getting outside too, I suggest you use an air purifier or a scrubber or, ideally, both. Use a Hepa air purifier, as these not only work on getting rid of odors, but also clean 99.9% of all molds in the air as well, which is great for an indoor garden. Make sure, though, that your air purifier is not an Ion one, as it will cause harm to your plants. Running an Ion air purifier outside the garden, on the other hand, is ok. You can find a good selection of air purifiers at any hardware store. A scrubber does the same thing as an air purifier by taking in smelly air and releasing clean air, but you can make one yourself that is twice as powerful. I like to make a scrubber when my bud is hanging to dry, since that is the worst time for odor. I take one of my charcoal filters and duct tape one of the exhaust fans directly to it on top. This will create a high power scrubber and will leave you with the better results than using an air purifier from a store.

## ■ Pest control and checking

There are four types of insects that are most likely to be a problem in an indoor gar-

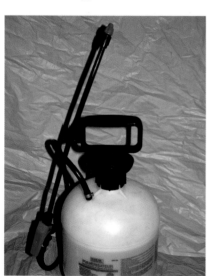

den: gnats, whitefly, thrips, and, the most common, spider mites. If you followed the room designs in this book, the only way you should get bugs is by bringing them into your garden yourself. This can happen if you bring a plant that is already infected from someone else's garden into yours. To avoid this, its very important to spray clones from someone else's garden with pesticide soap. For best results, go out and purchase a pump sprayer to apply it correctly. Follow the dosage on the bottle and spray each plant from top to bottom, being sure to get underneath the leaves. Some growers just dip the

clone in the soap but I find this too harsh; the clone then takes a long time to recover. I also suggest buying a brand name pesticide soap for better results. My favorite product is End All II by Safers.

If you find bugs in your crop, spray the plants immediately with the pump sprayer and pesticide soap. Start from the bottom of the plant, using one hand to massage and lift up the leaves of the plant while spraying at the same time, getting underneath all of the leaves until you make your way to the top. Spider mites lay their eggs underneath the leaves so it is very important to deal with the whole leaf.

There are some rules to follow when spraying your plants: never put your plants back under the lights until they are fully dried. If you put them straight back under light, they will fry. Also, wait at least two weeks before spraying the plants a second or third time. Finally, if you had to spray the plants well into flowering, wash the soap off with plain water and a pump sprayer before you harvest.

Every time you go to hand-feed your plants, carefully check the bottom leaves of the plant for bugs. This allows you to get at the problem as soon as possible and will hopefully avoid a big infestation. Checking for insects is what separates the men from the boys in indoor growing, and it must be done at all times for every crop you grow. Disinfecting the entire grow space in between grows with bleach—the walls, ceilings, everything—will help prevent them from coming back.

## ■ Molds

If you keep proper temperature and humidity and have no standing water in your garden, then mold should not be an issue. I'm sure you have heard of situations in which illegal grow ops destroyed homes due to mold. We are professional growers with professional gardens, not hack job artists, so this should be a non-issue. However, don't become complacent; the problem is so common that, for example, my home insurance covers my garden completely except for molds. As I mentioned earlier, the best defense against molds is a Hepa air purifier running in your garden 24 hours a day. Mold can also occur when hanging your bud to dry if your bud is too big, but this issue is easily taken care of by having decent air circulation in the room.

## ■ Powdery Mildew

Powdery mildew is the nastiest problem I have ever had to deal with. It appears as a white mold on top of your leaves and bud. Again, with the techniques shown in this book the only way you should get powdery mildew is by bringing it in the garden yourself. Here's how to deal with it:

### Step 1

Spray the plants with a sulfur solution using a pump sprayer. You will be able to find a sulfur solution in your grow store or garden center. This will remove the mildew.

### Step 2

Get a sulfur burner with sulfur pellets and let it burn for an hour once a week. Re-

member to turn off all fans first. For best results, do this when the lights are off. Do not use the sulfur burner within one week of harvest or you could end up with a sulfur taste and burn on your bud.

### Step 3

After the crop is finished, place every single piece of growing equipment (including water bucket, hose, etc.) in the garden. Run the sulfur burner for three hours a day, every day for at least two weeks. This should completely remove the powdery mildew problem.

## ■ Root and stem disease

With the feeding techniques shown in this book, root disease should not be an issue. If you're concerned about it, there are measures you can take. After every two weeks of feeding it's a good idea to clean the pots and roots out. To do this, just feed them plain water; for extra safety you can add a root cleaner solution to the water. This will help prevent and remove any root disease that may occur. My favorite product for this is called SM90, but there should be all kinds of root cleaners in your grow store to choose from.

Stem disease is usually an irreparable problem. It manifests as a bluish gooey substance decaying the main stalk or branches. All you can do at this point is cut off the branch or, if it's in the main stalk, cut out the infected area and hope for the best. Don't be too worried as stem disease is very rare and most likely you will never see it.

# Chapter 10

# Security and Safety

## ■ Hidden gardens

When growing marijuana indoors, in an urban environment, the security and safety of you, your family, and your home is crucial. This is true whether you are a legal medical grower or not, as it's not just the law that growers have to worry about; thieves don't care if your grow is legal or not, and if word gets out that you are growing marijuana in your home, you are at risk. In this chapter we will look at many techniques that will keep your garden the best-kept secret in your neighborhood.

If possible, having your garden in a hidden room is highly beneficial; it will help relieve stress and tension if someone you do not know has to enter your home, such as a repairman, or even a friend. The fewer people know about your garden, the better. It takes some more work to build a hidden garden, and a bit more money to run, but your safety—and being able to live with as little fear as possible in your home— is priceless. A hidden garden must be hidden both inside and out.

Start with the inside: the entrance to your garden should be a mystery to anyone standing right by it. (We're assuming an entrance that is inside your house, not outside, which wouldn't be wise.) This is easier than you may think; you just have to be creative. The best way to achieve this is to make the illusion that there is no entrance to your garden, just a solid wall. To do this, first remove the door to the garden and make a solid cover to go in its place. The cover must be made from the same material as the wall, so it will blend in with it. Paneling of any kind works amazingly well in disguising your entrance, as the seams of the paneling are very easy to hide; just cut the material to the same shape as your entrance, removing any trim you might have had around the door. Take a six- to twelve-inch thick piece of Styrofoam and attach it to the back of your cover using carpenters glue. The Styrofoam should fit exactly in your entrance, allowing no air or light to seep through the hidden

*This bud is from the lower branches on a Red Devil (Afghani x Afghani Skunk) plant.*

cover. You can use weather stripping to keep it tight and hold it well in place. If you do not have paneling on your wall, or cannot put paneling on your outside wall, a dark-colored paint will work well, too.

You have to be able to open your secret entrance. To do so, attach a small handle at eye-level and centered on the outside of the cover. To hide this handle, simply hang a painting or piece of art over it. All you have to do to get in the garden is remove the painting from the handle and pull out the cover to set aside until your work in the garden is done. Always remember to put it back on when finished! It's also important to cover any vents, but this is easy: simply put a cold air return cover over any intake or outtake holes that are exposed. Using dark colors for your vent cover works best. This does not block airflow and anyone who sees it will think it's just part of the house. If you have venting going to the outside, just do the same thing but use outdoor vent covers. You can also plant some bushes in front of the outdoor cover if it's low to the ground, to help keep it inconspicuous. Anyone who sees it will think it's just an air conditioner or dryer vent.

## ■ Light leakage

Once your garden is up and running, you need to thoroughly check both inside and outside your home for any light leakage. The 1,000-watt lights are very powerful and if there are any small cracks, they will show through clearly. If you notice any cracks, cover them using black and white poly, but if you followed the room designs I gave you, this shouldn't be necessary. The only light leaking to the outside should be from the outtake vent. Depending on the duct that leads outside, the light could seep through. To stop this, wrap the duct with black and white poly from inside your garden all the way to the outside wall.

## ■ Noise reduction techniques

Following the room designs given earlier in the book will take care of most of the noise that might come from your garden. Just in case, remember that the noise comes mainly from the intake or outtake fans. These fans are very powerful and push and pull a lot of air. Always use bungee cords to hang an exhaust fan, as this will deal with any noise or vibrations. For the vents, wrap insulation around all of your ductwork, then wrap plastic wrap over the top of the insulation. This will reduce at least three quarters of the airflow noise. You can buy duct that is already insulated, but of course it will cost you more money than regular duct.

## ■ Cameras and alarms

If you are going to grow marijuana in your home, I strongly suggest installing a security alarm. I feel more relaxed in my home with the plants knowing I have the

*Here is a full bud of Red Devil, from the main stalk of the plant, which is called a cola.*

alarm if trouble occurs. I also feel that if someone sees a sign or sticker on your home displaying that there is an alarm system installed, it makes them think twice about invading. These alarm systems also detect fires, which can help you minimize the damage to your home if a small fire does occur. You can also get alarms for room temperature as well; if the room reaches a high temperature, the alarm will go off, telling you that something has failed in the garden and it requires your immediate attention. These units will also tell you your current room temperature, which reduces the amount of regular room checks you will have to make.

I only suggest using cameras if your garden is not at your home but at another location. If you have a camera system in your home, you are basically saying to the public that you are up to something illegal, or at least that you have something worth protecting. If your garden is at a different location, however, they can be very useful. Most camera setups can run over the internet or right to your cell phone. Since you are not always at that location, being able to see that everything is running properly in the garden will give you peace of mind and reduce unnecessary trips. Having to visit your garden less also increases its security. Most setups have a motion detector as well, and will alert you if there is any activity so that you can address the problem as soon as possible. To get a good picture of your garden, place the camera high above the light shades; if the camera is exposed directly to HPS bulbs it will be hard to view your picture.

## ■ Garden checks

When your garden is up and running, the only work to be done in the garden is to feed the plants for half an hour every two to three days. The rest of your job is to babysit your garden as much as you can, as anything can go wrong with an indoor garden at any time. The sooner you are on top of the problem, the less damage will occur. For example, if an exhaust fan fails or a duct comes off the fan, a fully insulated garden is going to turn into an oven quickly. The plants will start to overheat, causing them major stress, plus the equipment in the room was not designed to run in temperatures of 110° F or higher, so could cause a fire.

As mentioned earlier, the conditions in your growing environment decide whether your final bud is substandard or very high quality. It's important to check every day that all the equipment is working properly and that the temperature and humidity are stable. Use the high and low function on the thermostat to monitor what happened while the lights were off and if any adjustments are needed. By making regular checks on the garden, you will prevent any chance of serious damage to your plants, home, and most importantly, yourself.

## ■ Equipment failure

Equipment can fail at any time, which is why it is so important for you to babysit

*Extrema is an indica-dominant ChemD x Herijuana hybrid, and is extremely strong. I got this from the fantastic Sannie's Seeds.*

your garden as much as possible. Most problems will just require a simple fix like re-attaching a piece of duct that has fallen off, or replacing a burned-out light bulb. The high and low thermostats will let you know if a piece of equipment fails, as they will show an abnormally high or low temperature in your garden. Check that the exhaust fans, ductwork, lights, air conditioner, and dehumidifier are all working properly every time you check the garden. If there is an equipment failure that causes the garden to overheat, but you cannot fix it that day, shut down the garden completely for the rest of the day. You can always make that day back; do not let your garden to continue to run. This will stop the stress on your plants immediately and your home will not be at risk.

## ■ Dos and don'ts while living with marijuana plants

Living with marijuana plants can be very dangerous, and you should always be concerned about their safety and yours. Use common sense at all times; your garden is a big responsibility. Avoid telling anyone that you grow marijuana; only tell someone if you have no other choice. You will have a great desire to show off your plants to all of your friends, but you must never do this. If you want to be "the man" and let everyone know you're the best, your reign as "the man" will be a short one. I know this totally sucks, but unfortunately, keeping your grow secret is in your best interests. Be careful about who you let into your home as well; do not throw open parties and, again, use common sense. If you have to have work done on your home, try to do it in between crops, or when you are in the early stages of production. If you have an emergency and you have to call a repairman to your home, don't freak out—they show up at grow ops all the time. Just remember one thing: NEVER SHOW YOUR GARDEN TO ANYONE, ANYTIME. If they know you grow, that is one thing, but giving them a full visual of your garden will be something they never forget. No matter how friendly they are and how many times they ask to see your garden, hold your ground and say no.

You must also be careful bringing supplies and equipment into and out of your place. Make sure everything is concealed; use garbage bags if you have to. If you get caught bringing in bales of soil or growing lights into your home, the neighbors will probably work it out. As long as you follow these tips and all the other instructions in this book, you and your home should be safe.

## ■ Safety equipment

When it comes to safety equipment, a fire in the garden is your biggest concern. Make sure you have a fire alarm inside the garden and outside it, near the entrance as well. Also, always have a fire extinguisher both inside and outside of your garden too; make sure they are rated for electrical fires. Your local grow store might stock

fire extinguishers that attach to the ceiling and will spray if smoke is detected. You also need to protect your eyes: the 1,000-watt lights will cause damage, so wear sunglasses at all times and safety glasses when trimming during harvest.

In terms of personal safety, I do not condone guns at all, and if your grow is illegal, having a gun on the property is a very, very stupid idea. A bat can be enough to intimidate a would-be intruder, and a big, mean-sounding dog could prevent the situation from even happening. A big dog is also a great protector for your home when you're not there.

# Chapter 11

# Choosing Your Strains

## ■ Sativas

There are two main species (genotype) of marijuana - sativa and indica – and hybrids of the two are very abundant. Each variety, whether pure or a hybrid, has a different effect (high) and plant structure. Sativa strains are my personal favorite. Good sativas give what I call "working weed": a powerful, uplifting, energized effect that helps you keep alert and find the energy that you are lacking. The high tends to be more cerebral than a strong body buzz, which can leave you with little energy. I like to be active during the day and maintain some productivity, so I always start my morning with a good sativa, which gives me a little kick and some focus, making me lighter on my feet. I have met artists, for example, who cannot work artistically on marijuana, but once I've introduced them to a nice sativa, their creative juices start flowing. Also, my brain has metal poisoning, so the strong cerebral effect relieves my pain and keeps my thoughts focused and collected, allowing me to have a normal day just like anyone else. If it was not for sativa strains I would not have been able to write this book.

Sativas are often taller plants with thinner stalks, which are very easy to stretch while in the garden. To tell if you have a sativa, look at the fan leaves on the plants; the skinnier the fan leaf fingers, the more sativa is in your plant. I suggest experimenting with a Haze-style plant, which will be guaranteed to have strong sativa properties. You will notice that the fan leaf fingers are quite skinny on a Haze plant.

## ■ Indicas

Indicas are the opposite of sativas, and for most people, carry more medicinal properties. An indica stone has a very strong full-body effect, which relieves severe body pain.

A good indica will have an overwhelming
effect on your body, sometimes leaving
you unable to move from the couch
(known as "couch-lock"). If you have work
to do, I suggest you do not use a strong indica strain, but if you are very sick and in a
lot of pain, a good indica will take care of
your problems and give you a good chance
of having a normal day. On the street, indicas are better sellers because of their overwhelming effects. To find out if your plant
is an indica, check the fingers of your fan
leaves: they will be wide and fat. The wider the fingers, the more indica is in the plant.
Indicas in most cases also will be a bushier, shorter style of plant with a thicker stalk.

## ■ Hybrids

A hybrid is basically what you get when you cross a sativa with an indica, or vice
versa. Depending on the genes of the strain, your plant will have a certain percentage of sativa and a certain percentage of indica. With hundreds and hundreds of
strains out there, it is likely that your plant will be a hybrid instead of a pure indica
or sativa. This is what makes the different strains unique, as each has its own special mix of medicinal properties. To tell how much sativa and indica is in your plants,
again, look at the fingers of your fan leaves: if the fingers are a little skinnier than
a normal leaf, then you have what we call "mostly sativa"; if your fingers are fatter
than a normal leaf, then you have what we call "mostly indica."

## ■ How to gauge the effects of a strain

The strain that you choose to grow will depend upon what medicinal properties you require from your bud. This can be an extreme high, or an extreme low, or a combination of both. For instance, I have used a famous strain known as Blueberry, which was mostly sativa, giving me a boost and the head relief I was looking for, but it still had 20% indica in it for my body, which did not require the same attention that my head needed. If you go in to a medical marijuana dispensary, there will be a simple scale for you to look at for each strain, telling you what percentage of indica and sativa is in the strain. If the scale leans more towards indica, then you know you are getting a more relaxing body effect. If the scale leans more towards sativa, then you will be looking at a more uplifting, cerebral effect. If you purchase seeds from a seed company, they will tell you if it is mostly indica or sativa, and you can make your decision based upon that. Unfortunately, when buying seeds that are hybrids, there is no way to tell the ratio of genetics. A set of ten plants grown from the same set of seeds often have widely different characteristics, just as your brothers and sisters will have a different genetic mix, even though you share the same parents. After the vegetative process you will be able to tell the sativa/indica mixture of your plants by the structure and thickness of the stalk, as well as the fingers on your fan leaves.

## ■ Using the internet

The internet is the best tool there is to find information about strains. When looking for a strain, I suggest you research the marijuana seed companies. On their websites they should have a complete breakdown of each strain they carry. They mention the following: flowering period, sativa/indica combination, origin, breeder, smell, taste, and a brief explanation of the strain's qualities. When I try a new strain, I find out who carried the strain first, and then check the info from everyone who sells it. This info should be the same for each company; sometimes it's the same exact information, word for word. This is the most reliable source of information on the strain you can get. There are marijuana review sites that give you the same info plus the author's opinion on the strain, as well, and this may be useful to you. The problem, though, is that the reviewer is not an expert and is just giving his personal opinion. Also, as mentioned earlier, who knows what version (or 'phenotype', the use the proper term) of the plant the reviewer has. There are also marijuana strain databases, on which there is information about hundreds of strains. Most of the time these sites are correct, but double-check with the main seed company to ensure the information is very similar. The best place to get the information is from the actual breeder, although this is not always possible. I do suggest that you stay away from the marijuana forum sites. The information you find there can be very mixed, and most of the people on them are

just as confused as you are. Also, these sites can be misleading as you may be growing a different phenotype than the one you're reading about.

I will list some of my favorite sites so you can begin the search for strains. If you have no idea what strain you want, start with the marijuana databases and review sites. Once you have made your decision, find out which seed companies sell them and use their info to do more research. If you have a strain that you did not purchase over the internet, which was given to you with no information, then start by searching the seed companies first and then check out the reviews. If you have a strain in mind, then Google "(name of strain)" + "marijuana seeds" and that should lead you to the actual breeder and sites to purchase seeds from.

## ■ Medical marijuana strain web sites

- medicalmarijuanastrains.com
- dope-seeds.com/medical_marijuana.htm
- findmypot.com
- marijuanastrains.com
- universityofseeds.com
- weedbay.net
- marijuanareviews.com
- strainreviews.net

# Chapter 12

# How Should You Use Medical Marijuana?

In this chapter, I am going to show you how I used (and still use) medical marijuana. Medical marijuana was a major key to surviving my illness for eight years while suffering from severe metal poisoning every day. Imagine an intense food poisoning that never goes away, and you can understand my situation. Becoming a legal grower was a factor to my success, but if it was not for the consistent quality of my marijuana and how tactfully I used it, I would never have made it. I hope these methods will give you an idea about how to go about using medical marijuana for your own situation.

## ■ Inhalation

### Marijuana cigarettes (joints)

Marijuana cigarettes are by far the most popular and commonly used form of inhaling marijuana. You place the chopped up marijuana on a cigarette rolling paper, then roll it up, lick the glue, and light it up and smoke it like a normal cigarette. If you are going to use medical marijuana every day (and this applies especially to chronically ill people who will have to use it for the rest of their lives), this is the most unhealthy, wasteful, and ineffective way of using medical marijuana. You will use more marijuana to fill the cigarette than you would in other, more effective ways of medicating. Also, almost half of the smoke will be released into the air during the time between inhales. A regular-sized marijuana cigarette has a weak draw, which does not use the marijuana to its full potential, and will leave you needing to medicate more often. This will do serious damage to your medical marijuana supply. It is also the unhealthiest way you could take your marijuana, due to there being no filtration at all, and it encourages excessive use as it is not as long lasting or as effective as other methods.

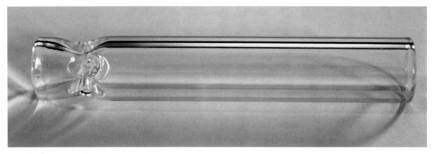

### Straight shooter (one hitter)

A straight shooter, or one-hitter, is a pipe shaped like a cigarette; in fact, most straight shooters are disguised to look like a normal cigarette. The problem with them is that you only get one hit and the airflow is the same as in a joint. The best glass straight shooters have the space to give you half a dozen hits with a large enough airflow to be very effective. This tool is great for re-energizing a previous high or for situations where you need relief but cannot be extremely disoriented. It is also good for use outdoors and when traveling since it is easy to conceal and just takes seconds to fill and inhale.

Take your chopped or ground marijuana and stuff the smaller end of the pipe.

Make sure you stuff it tight so it will not fall out while inhaling. Use a lighter or match to burn the marijuana while inhaling on the opposite end. Repeat steps until there is no longer any smoke traveling through the pipe.

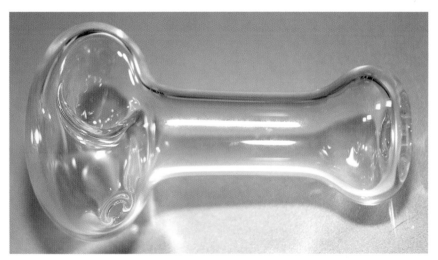

### Regular hand pipe

A hand pipe is another cheap, effective tool that uses small amounts of marijuana and, like the straight shooter, gives you decent relief, but which does not leave you too blasted to do other important things. They are made from all kinds of materials, such as metal, glass, Pyrex, soap stone and ceramics. I personally always buy glass pipes as I find they deliver the smoothest hit, but any kind will deliver the same punch. Like the straight shooter, a hand pipe does not have any filtration, so I do not recommend it for regular use. To use, just stuff the bowl of the pipe with

chopped or ground marijuana, then light the bowl while you inhale on the other end. Repeat this process until you can no longer draw smoke.

### Bubbler

Bubblers are great as they filter marijuana smoke and are a good way to medicate. A bubbler is a handheld glass pipe that has a small reservoir, which you fill with water beneath the bowl holding the chopped or ground marijuana. The smoke travels directly through the reservoir from the burning bowl, then travels through the stem and into your lungs. The water in the reservoir filters out any toxins or tar resin in the smoke before it hits your lungs. This gives a healthier and cleaner smoke. Bubblers have a bigger stem, allowing more airflow of smoke to reach the lungs, and giving a more powerful and longer lasting effect.

They are known as bubblers because when you draw from the pipe, the little reservoir of water makes a strong bubbling noise. A bubbler will also have what we call a

carburetor. You must cover the carburetor hole on the pipe when drawing your smoke. When your lungs are almost filled with smoke, you release your finger from the carburetor to allow air into the pipe, sending what smoke is still left in the pipe into your lungs. When your finger is not on the carburetor, the air prevents it from pulling smoke from the bowl. Some people know this hole as the "choke". If you do not have the strongest lungs, and want the most bang for your buck, then a bubbler is the way to go.

## Water bong

When I was going through the roughest years of my illness, the water bong was my weapon of choice. To me, it is the heaviest way of medicating yourself. A water bong works the same way as a bubbler, but has a much larger water reservoir and stem to allow more smoke to enter your lungs at once. If you're a first-time bong user, I suggest that you buy a clear bong first. Being able to see the smoke travel through the pipe will allow you to gauge how much you should inhale at once, preventing you from coughing up a lung and over medicating yourself. Just like the bubbler, smoke goes from the burning bowl through the water reservoir, then through the stem and into your lungs. The bigger the water reservoir, the cleaner and more powerful the smoke will be.. After some use of the bong, you will see buildup of resin

that was prevented from entering your lungs.

There are two different styles of carburetor for a water bong. Some will be above the reservoir, just like the bubbler, but most water bongs require you to pull out the bowl to allow air into the pipe, clearing what's left into your lungs and preventing new smoke from being drawn. If you're a beginner, I don't suggest doing this all at once. Take your initial draw, then cover the stem with your hand and exhale before clearing the rest of the bong. Place your hand over the top to stop any smoke escaping; once the smoke comes in contact with the air it will become very foul and harsh. Using a water bong or a bubbler, you will get through just half the amount you would use in a joint, and receive twice the power and length of effect. This will make your stash last much longer, and let's not forget the amount of tar and toxins that are prevented from entering your body.

### Dual chamber water bong

A dual chamber water bong is used in much the same way as a regular water bong, the only difference being that the smoke filters through two reservoirs of water before going through the stem and into your lungs. As I mentioned earlier, the more water for the smoke to filter through, the cleaner the smoke. With a dual chamber

there is more water to filter smoke, but the purpose of the second chamber is actually to remove resin and toxins from the smoke. If you fill the first chamber (the one with the burning bowl attached) with hot water and the second chamber with cold water, close to 91% of resin and toxins will be removed from the smoke. This is the cleanest form of medicating yourself that I am aware of that involves combustion. For an even smoother draw, you can fill the stem with ice cubes; this can be done with a regular water bong as well.

### Vaporizer (Volcano)

There are many vaporizers on the market today; they all work, but the only one that works perfectly and can take years of daily abuse is the Volcano, which is made in Germany and is available both on the internet and any head shop in the world. The best way to describe a vaporizer is that it is a device that cooks, not burns, your marijuana.

Once the marijuana hits a certain temperature, it releases a smoke-free vapor.

You put your chopped or ground marijuana in the cartridge, then place the screen on top. There is a plastic bag that you attach to the marijuana-filled cartridge. Turn on the volcano and set a desired temperature. When the volcano reaches that temperature a light will go off, telling you it is ready. You then turn on the blower switch, which blows the smokeless vapor into the bag. Once the bag is full, turn off the blower switch, detach the bag from the cartridge, add a mouthpiece to the bag, and finally inhale the bag of vapor. Once you have filled the bag

you will be able to tell what temperature to set the volcano in future. If the bag is completely clear, your temperature is too low; if the bag is full of smoke, the temperature is too high; you should be able to see the vapor but still see clearly through

the bag. The ideal temperature will depend on how dry your marijuana is. In most cases the temperature should be around 374 degrees Fahrenheit, and the classic version of the Volcano should be set around six. The volcano has been thoroughly

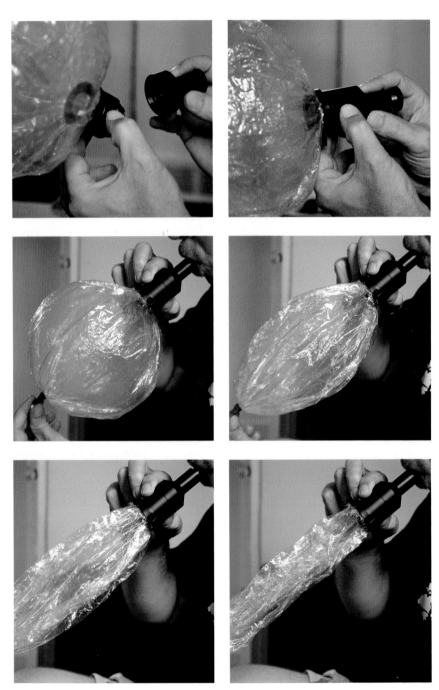

tested at major universities and is the cleanest form of inhaling marijuana, with a 99.9% tar and toxin removal rate. It is also very powerful; do not use with a strong sativa if you plan on going to bed within three hours.

## ■ Digesting

Digesting food made with medical marijuana is also a very effective way of medicating, and gives those who do not want to inhale smoke a healthier alternative. You can make almost any food with marijuana, from baked goods to spaghetti sauce to ice cream to soda pop. There are many medical marijuana recipes in books and on the internet. Most people tend to first make medical marijuana butter, and then cook with this as you would cook with normal butter. It is fairly easy to make, and you can make enough butter to last months from just one crop. It can also be frozen. Cooking with straight marijuana can be very unappetizing; cooking with butter best disguises the taste. The other great benefit of cooking with medical marijuana is you can use your waste from harvest. All of the leaf and trimmings that were pulled and cut from harvest can be broken down into excellent edibles.

To best utilize this waste, take all the leaf and trimmings from your harvest and dry them out completely. Put it all in a garbage bag and crush it up with your hands until it is all shake. Take three pounds of real butter and boil it down in a pot. Put a minimum of half a pound of your readymade dry shake into the pot with the boiling butter. Boil the butter and the shake together for a minimum of two hours, stirring every twenty minutes. When finished, take a strainer and pour the pot butter through it into a plastic container; put this in the fridge to harden for a couple of days, and you're ready to cook. My favorite thing to do with the butter is make shortbread or peanut butter cookies; you can make dozens with just one pound of medical marijuana butter.

Digesting marijuana has a different effect than inhaling. Once digested it can take up to forty minutes to an hour before you feel the full effects. I find that I then get a heavy body buzz, which lasts an hour or two longer than when it's inhaled. This is an excellent choice for those who are trying to relieve physical pain.

## ■ Topical

Another way to use medical marijuana is topically, on the skin. This is very effective for muscle and joint pains. Marijuana can be found as a balm, lotion, ointment, or a simple alcohol solution, and can be purchased or made simply at home. The simplest way of making a medical marijuana topical product from home is the alcohol solution. Take an eighth of dry chopped or ground bud, put inside a half empty bottle of ISO or rubbing alcohol, and leave it in the fridge for a week, shaking it up really hard each day. It can be messy when you go to rub it on your skin if you do not strain it, but it's more effective if you leave the plant matter in the bottle.

When using a topical solution, just as when ingesting medical marijuana, you can expect to feel the effects from 40 minutes to an hour after application. Be aware that you will receive no physical or cerebral high whatsoever; it simply relieves muscle and joint pain where applied to your body.

# ■ When and what to use to medicate

### Body pain

When trying to relieve chronic body pain, choosing a pure or mostly-indica strain will be the most effective. For body pain, you will need to use a strong tool, like a water bong or vaporizer, for total relief. Ingesting medical marijuana is also a very good solution for severe and daily body pain. I only suggest using a topical solution for centralized body pain, like a strained wrist or lower back pain; inhaling or ingesting is the best way to relieve your entire body.

### Ups and downs

I suffer both physically and mentally, and find myself either too high or too low in my physical or mental state, depending on the day. To make sure I have a normal, productive day, I will break from my normal medicating process and address whichever problem is most prominent at that time. If I'm too high mentally and physically, I will knock myself down with a pure or mostly indica, using a weaker tool to inhale like the straight shooter or small hand pipe. If that doesn't do the trick, I will either repeat that process again immediately or move up to a water bong or vaporizer.

When I am really low physically or mentally, I go in the opposite direction by using a strong sativa or Haze strain. Again, I start small using a straight shooter or small hand pipe; I only move up to a water bong or vaporizer when I am still too low to get on with my day. Remember not to over medicate!

### Working

If you have to work using medical marijuana, a pure or mostly-sativa strain is the only way to go. Indicas are too heavy, especially physically, whereas a sativa should be uplifting and energetic. The trick to working when on medical marijuana is to find the relief you need without being unable to think straight. This is when I use the straight shooter most: it gets me to where I want to be so I can work, but does not leave me so disoriented that I am useless. I also use smaller, weaker pieces of less potent bud – you can always take more but you can't take less. This not only makes me productive, it also enhances my working capabilities and train of thought.

### Cerebral

Using a pure sativa or Haze with a vaporizer is the best choice for those who suffer from head pain. A sativa has a strong cerebral effect, giving you instant relief where you need it. In most cases, when people suffer from head trauma, the pain is severe, so a vaporizer or water bong will be needed to treat the problem fully. I find that vaporizer is best for targeting the brain directly.

## ■ Making a medical marijuana usage plan

Everyone's daily suffering is different. I am going to explain how I use medical marijuana daily to hopefully give you some direction in making your own daily usage plan. I treat medical marijuana the same way as I treat my other medication; I try to get medicated at the exact same time of day, each day. This will give you more stability for your daily activities—the more routine, the better. You will also need a strong strain and a mild strain to cover all situations. Once you have made your selections, stick with them. If you are suffering from manic depression, for example, your doctor is not going to prescribe you Prozac one day, then Zoloft the next day, then Paxil the next. Yes, all of these drugs treat manic depression, but for them to work to their fullest they cannot be mixed or just taken randomly each day. I know everyone likes variety, but if you are chronically ill, a strict routine is the best method for your body to heal and stay adjusted for daily life.

My daily routine goes like this: I start my day with a light toke using the straight shooter with a good sativa. Every two or three hours throughout the day I will repeat the same process. This keeps me productive and able to think clearly when I need it the most. When my day is done, normally around 4:20 pm, I will give my head some full relief by using that same sativa in a water bong or vaporizer. Later in the evening, I will switch to my indica for a low, and begin the process of shutting down so I can not only get to sleep later but have a full rest throughout the night. I will use a vaporizer in the early evening with my indica which still helps me keep lifted for the evening, and then I will use a strong water bong to put myself to bed.

# Index